THEATER AND REVOLUTION IN FRANCE SINCE 1968

FRENCH FORUM MONOGRAPHS

4

Editors R.C. LA CHARITÉ and V.A. LA CHARITÉ

THEATER AND REVOLUTION IN FRANCE SINCE 1968

by
JUDITH GRAVES MILLER

FRENCH FORUM, PUBLISHERS
LEXINGTON, KENTUCKY

Library of Congress Catalog Card Number 76-47500

ISBN 0-917058-03-8

Printed in the United States of America

----

to my parents

ACKNOWLEDGEMENTS

I am grateful for the assistance of the College of Wooster in the preparation of this manuscript. I wish, in particular, to thank those professors who have always encouraged my work: Ilse Lipschutz of Vassar College; Bernard Schilling and Fernande Gontier of the University of Rochester; Michel Rybalka of Washington University.

Most of all I thank the actors, technicians, directors, writers, and critics of French theater who offered me their ideas, their hospitality, and the chance to share their experience: Robert Abirached, The Aquarium, André Benedetto and the Nouvelle Compagnie d'Avignon, Aimé Césaire, Emile Copfermann, Anne-Marie Duguet, Benouali Laribi, Marcel Maréchal, Georges Michel, Sophie Lemasson and the Théâtre du Soleil, the Salamandre, the Théâtre Populaire de Lorraine, and the Troupe des 7 Mendiants.

PREFACE

«May 1968» in France not only convulsed the university and upset the economy but also wrought havoc in the cultural domain. Particularly affected by the month-long period of strikes and street demonstrations, the French stage became a focal point of protest. Actors, directors, revolutionary theorists, and theater critics reopened with a vengeance the debate on the role of theater in society. While radical groups performed agit-prop skits on public squares or in factories to spur on the «Revolution,» adherents of the twenty-year-old popular theater movement gathered in Villeurbanne to examine the results of «cultural democratization.» Discovering the *non-public*, they deemed their efforts to bring culture to the workers a failure.

Shaken playwrights and directors, in the aftermath of May, produced a series of introspective plays which decried the theater's political impotence. At the other end of the psychological spectrum, a half dozen small troupes, born out of the May events or radicalized by the political insights May afforded, dedicated themselves to carrying out the work of the aborted rebellion. They strove to combine the goals of popular theater (thus reducing the *non-public*) with a protest against the political status quo. Moreover, they married their leftist orientation to formal experimentation in order to produce a revolutionary theater which encompassed both government overthrow and esthetic innovation. «Audience participation,» «collective creation,» «improvisation,» «environmental theater» became key terms in their professional idiom. Finally, their socialist philosophy, extended to their troupe structure, brought about a «revolution» in the theatrical institution.

Theater and Revolution in France Since 1968 discusses the background of post-May revolutionary theater: the popular theater movement (particularly since its renaissance in the late 1940's), the discovery of Bertolt Brecht in France, the influence of Antonin Artaud, and the May crisis itself, and then examines the work of four troupes which exemplify contemporary French «revolutionary theater»: the Théâtre du Soleil, the Aquarium, the Théâtre Populaire de Lorraine, and André Benedetto's La Nouvelle Compagnie d'Avignon. All four of these troupes have taken up the political challenge of Bertolt Brecht while aspiring to create «la poésie de l'espace» demanded by Antonin Artaud. Attracting working-class audiences to their low-priced productions, they keep alive the popular theater movement which a lack of government support has seriously endangered. They manage, despite constant financial strains, to face the dilemma of subsidy or subversion without compromising their artistic quality or their political goals.

TABLE OF CONTENTS

PREFACE 9

I. WHAT IS REVOLUTIONARY THEATER? 13

II. THEATER AND REVOLUTION: 20
A BACKGROUND 1945-1968

III. MAY '68 AND THE THEATER 32

IV. THEATRE DU SOLEIL: THEATER AS 52
REVOLUTION, REVOLUTION AS THEATER

V. ANDRE BENEDETTO: RITUAL AND 76
REVOLUTION

VI. THEATRE POPULAIRE DE LORRAINE: 97
REGIONAL THEATER

VII. THE AQUARIUM: AT WAR WITH 115
«LA REPUBLIQUE DES HONNETES GENS»

VIII. THE IMPACT OF CONTEMPORARY 137
REVOLUTIONARY THEATER

NOTES 145

BIBLIOGRAPHY 156

Chapter I

WHAT IS REVOLUTIONARY THEATER?

> Si la pratique du théâtre peut aujourd'hui [...] avoir un
> sens, c'est à travers la générosité que peuvent apporter des
> hommes de théâtre à le mettre au service du combat révolu-
> tionnaire. L'important n'est pas d'être fidèle à telle rhétori-
> que fondée sur l'enseignement d'Artaud ou de Brecht mais
> de retrouver, pour nourrir en nous le feu, ce qui fait en défi-
> nitive leur commune volonté, qui est volonté de révolution,
> plus strictement politique chez l'un plus précisément inspi-
> rée de la révolte de Rimbaud chez l'autre.
>
> Gilles Sandier, *Théâtre et combat*
> (Paris: Stock, 1970), p. 357.

Theater is a witness of its time, an image of its epoch. It is also
the epoch's conscience and judge. Witness, it mirrors the reigning stability or instability in society and government. Judge, it
criticizes or condones prevailing ideologies.

Writing about theater and the twentieth century, Peter Brook
posits the necessity of a critical stance:

A stable and harmonious society might need only to look for ways of reflecting and reaffirming its harmony in its theatres. Such theatres could set

out to unite cast and audiences in a mutual 'yes.' But a shifting, chaotic world often must choose between a playhouse that offers a spurious 'yes' or a provocation so strong that it splinters its audience into fragments of vivid 'nos' (1).

Contemporary French theater, after the debacle of the May '68 «Revolution,» has opted for provocation. It responds «no» to present social and economic conditions, «no» to racism, to fascism, to repression. Concurrently, it refuses theatrical conformity, rejecting the well-made play, the italianate stage, the separation of actor and audience, and the hierarchical seating system. It is revolutionary theater in the dual sense of the term, both advocating political change and experimenting with formal possibilities.

As such, post-68 theater continues and, indeed, unites the two predominant theatrical currents of the twentieth century: politicization and «retheatricalization.» The transformation of theater into a political weapon, although hardly an invention of twentieth-century thespians, received new impetus in turn-of-the century experiments (2). Advocates of popular theater and cultural democratization opened theaters in the provinces and in the working-class districts of Paris in order to bring drama to the culturally deprived. The utopian socialist philosophy behind such efforts culminated in the government action which established the Théâtre National Populaire in 1920. While government used theater as a means of political integration, others, such as the Communist agit-prop group, «Octobre» (1929-1936), attempted to raise the political consciousness of the workers against the ruling class. The latter agreed with Erwin Piscator, whose Berlin workers' theater (1927-1929) paradoxically served as a model for many government subsidized popular theater ventures in the 1950's and 1960's.

Retheatricalization, or reinvesting theater with a ritual quality, has been the concern of playwrights and directors such as Lugné-Poë, Alfred Jarry, Jean-Paul Sartre, Jean Genet, and Roger Blin. From turn-of-the-century attempts by Lugné-Poë to revitalize theater by abolishing the notion of exact imitation to the recent physical excesses and vocal experimentation of the disciples of Antonin Artaud, theater professionals have attempted to reestablish theater's power to create myth.

The two major voices of contemporary theater, Antonin Artaud and Bertolt Brecht, devoted their creative and theoretical talents to a multi-dimensional revolutionary theater in which politicization and retheatricalization play major roles. Both rejected the inheritance of nineteenth-century bourgeois theater: «un théâtre qui utilise sans les modifier le système des croyances et les valeurs acceptées et qui ne remet point en cause l'image de la personne humaine communément admise» (3). Both were concerned with taking a new look at reality, shaking up man's consciousness, and freeing him from repression. However, each proposed a revolutionary model as different in its final goal as in its methods (4).

In revolt against «dead theater,» Artaud wanted theater to reveal life, to expose and liberate man's sexual powers and his vital energy. His theater would become a therapeutic device, reuniting exterior man with his hidden inner self and with the life force:

Une vraie pièce de théâtre bouscule le repos des sens, libère l'inconscient comprimé, pousse à une sorte de révolte virtuelle et qui d'ailleurs ne peut avoir tout son prix que si elle demeure virtuelle, impose aux collectivités rassemblées une attitude héroïque et difficile (5).

The revolution he proposed was not ideologically oriented, but geared to psychological and metaphysical liberation. Artaud was unconcerned with political forces. Although he stated that «L'état social est inique et bon à détruire» and that theater *should* be preoccupied with the social question, he added, «C'est encore plus [le fait] de la mitraille.» Theater has another object which is «plus hautain» and «plus secret» (6).

Marxist Bertolt Brecht, on the other hand, called for a socialist revolution and a theater which communicates to the audience the need for such a revolution:

We need a type of theater which not only releases the feelings, insights and impulses possible within the particular historical field of human relations in which the action takes place, but employs and encourages those thoughts and feelings which help transform the field itself (7).

Coinciding with the progressive themes of the century, Brecht's theories affirmed that art can and must intervene in history, for man is correctable and the world transformable. While for Artaud theater by itself could resolve human and supra-human conflict, for Brecht theater was meant to point the way to a social revolution outside dramatic confines.

Just as the revolutions proposed by Brecht and Artaud differ, so do the techniques devised to achieve them. Artaud would attack the spectator's senses rather than his intellect, surrounding him with spectacle, violent physical images, concrete music, cries, and chants. The spectators and actors become celebrants in a ritual they themselves create.

Brecht, however, valued above all the spectator's lucidity. In his dialectical dramas, the spectator's judgment is necessary to complete the play. Through the practice of *verfremdung*, or alienation effect, Brecht would reduce the emotional involvement of the public by inserting choral commentary, musical interludes, and projections between the loosely connected sequences of the play. He advocated an acting style in which the actor is not only in complete control of his character but also capable of stepping out of the character and criticizing him.

Despite these differences, both Artaud and Brecht brought to the forefront certain fundamental theatrical concerns that had long been put to rest in the West, in particular the sign value of actors and objects and the relationship of the actor to the audience. Both believed in a theater of formal perfection in which the content of the work calls forth the form of the expression. In addition, and in line with twentieth-century developments, Artaud and Brecht helped confirm the primacy of the director in the theatrical endeavor. They established his responsibility for analyzing and giving meaning to the play.

Artaud and Brecht have been instrumental in orienting contemporary French theatrical production. The former is best known for his techniques rather than for his theory of theater as therapeutic revolt. Indeed Artaud's metaphysical-anarchical revolution has very nearly disappeared. Happenings, which flourished in France in 1963-65, with the artist attempting to reach the collective unconscious, have been transformed into a kind of frenzied self-celebration, such as the work of Ben (Benjamin Vautier) and Jean-Pierre Bisson.

The «art is life» concept, or the attempt to make the theatrical experience the substance of life, now finds its foremost practitioner in the American Bob Wilson. When performed in France his inordinately long spectacles, with their sequences of esoteric images and hermetic meanings, have engendered a greater enthusiasm than in New York. They have had, however, scant influence on French theater practice. Wilson's «messianisme humble» (8) has not so far attracted Gallic disciples.

Brecht's influence has led to the politicization of contemporary French theater. His emphasis on politicized productions has affected the majority of young theater professionals; but his dramatic methods have generally been found unsuitable for French actors and audiences. Notable exceptions to this, however, include the work of directors Bernard Sobel and Jean-Pierre Vincent. Sobel is the most rigorous disciple of Brecht in France, utilizing in his productions the techniques of the Berlin Ensemble, with which he worked. While employing Brecht's epic style, Jean-Pierre Vincent deliberately chooses plays, including those of Brecht's «expressionistic» period, which were not originally conceived as epic productions. By submitting these to an epic treatment (use of the alienation effect, muted colors, character control, revalorization of objects), he demonstrates how the epic style casts a critical light on society.

Today theater professionals attempt to surpass both Brecht and Artaud through synthesis of the two. Since the upheavals of May '68, the tendency has been to combine the political orientation of Brecht with the formal experimentation of Artaud. Even those followers of Artaud who rely particularly on his concepts of celebration and rupture do not ignore the radicalization of political currents since 1968. Gérard Gélas, typical of contemporary disciples of Artaud, raises his public's political consciousness while deconditioning its accepted vision of the world:

C'est la porte ouverte à la révolution que de tenir entrebâillée celle du rêve, la prise de conscience politique est une étape, mais étape seulement. Elle doit se hisser au niveau des manifestations les plus exaltantes de l'existence (9).

He combines dream images and fantasmagorical visions with political discourse in an attempt to unify his spectators in a common revolt.

Jérome Savary and the Grand Magic Circus, an itinerant troupe traveling from city to city, unite audience and actors in a raucous festival satirizing contemporary society while aiming for momentary psychological liberation. Savary, contrary to Gélas, does not want to reform anything, but rather aid and abet the decomposition of the old world.

Four contemporary troupes which exemplify post-68 revolutionary theater by combining the lessons of Artaud and Brecht are the Théâtre du Soleil, the Aquarium, the Théâtre Populaire de Lorraine, and the Nouvelle Compagnie d'Avignon. The Théâtre du Soleil and the Aquarium, having reconstructed their theaters in an abandoned armaments factory in a Parisian suburb, practice collective creation and satirical contestation. While the Soleil borrows dramatic techniques from the Middle Ages and the *théâtre de foire*, including the public in the structure of its plays, the Aquarium experiments with documentary theater, appealing to its public's critical faculties. The Théâtre Populaire de Lorraine typifies a regional theater approach. Working out of Metz, it exposes the practices of the local iron and steel trusts to its working-class audience. Forsaking strictly regional problems, André Benedetto and his Avignon troupe, the Nouvelle Compagnie d'Avignon, dramatize class struggle and the Occitanian liberation movement. Benedetto's mystical persona transforms his productions into political rites.

Each of these groups has been marked by the intensification of political consciousness in France and the events of May '68. Each situates itself firmly in the tradition of *théâtre engagé*, while adding a pro-Marxist bias. None of them falls into the category of agit-prop or limited, purely propagandistic theater which advocates immediate political action. At times, however, they utilize agit-prop techniques.

They are not exclusively and nihilistically examining the

form of theater, declaring, as does the Paris-based Argentinian troupe, T.S.E., the impossibility of theater in contemporary society. But neither do they consider themselves a substitute for political parties. They therefore avoid the danger mentioned by theater critic Emile Copfermann: «Plaquer un discours révolutionnaire sur une forme théâtrale c'est être aussi efficace pour la politique et pour le théâtre qu'en cautérisant une jambe de bois» (10). These groups seek to integrate their political concern with a new style of theater; and in doing so they realize a revolution in the theatrical institution itself.

Chapter II

THEATER AND REVOLUTION: A BACKGROUND 1945-1968

> Don't be taken in
> when they pat you paternally on the shoulder and say
> that there's no inequality worth speaking of
> and no more reason
> for fighting
> Because if you believe them
> they will be completely in charge
> in their marble homes and granite banks
> from which they rob the people of the world
> under the pretense of bringing them culture.
> Marat, from Peter Weiss, *Marat/Sade*, trans. Geoffrey Skelton and
> Adrian Mitchell (London: Calder-Boyars, 1965), pp. 63-64.

Not since 1789 had the old debate on the role of theater in society been resurrected in France with as much force as after the
Second World War (1). Post-war union activism combined with
the ideals of the *union sacrée* of the Resistance helped revitalize
the notion of «popular theater.» Previously championed by
Jean Zay during his brief tenure as Minister of Education for
the Popular Front, «popular theater» illustrated the old republi-

can concept of a morally and socially educative theater. Opposed to the notion of proletarian art, advocates of popular theater hoped to unify all classes through their common cultural heritage. Those culturally unadapted would be educated to bourgeois standards.

In 1945, theater professionals found the Cartel's esthetic revolution (1919-1939) inadequate to answer the challenges of popular theater. They began equating change in theater with change in theater public. Well-known theatrical figures, including Pierre-Aimé Touchard, Jean-Marie Serreau, Charles Dullin, Jean-Louis Barrault, Jean Vilar, and Jean-Paul Sartre participated in colloquia designed to propose methods of bringing theater to the «people.» While Barrault and Roger Blin gave free acting courses to Parisian workers, others, such as Jean Dasté and Maurice Sarrazin, left Paris to set up regional theater in the provinces. The Communist Party created the association «Travail et Culture» to supply inexpensive tickets to the working class and encourage their theater attendance.

Following the professionals' lead, the government took up the popular theater cause in 1947. Jeanne Laurent, Sous-Directrice des Arts au Secrétariat des Arts et Lettres and chief proponent of decentralization, created the first subsidized provincial dramatic centers in St. Etienne, Toulouse, Rennes, and Strasbourg. She encouraged government action which established financial aid for first plays and young directors.

By 1950 government intervention in theater projects took on the amplitude of a *cause célèbre*. To ballast the State's involvement, Laurent appointed Jean Vilar to head the dormant Théâtre National Populaire. From 1951 to 1963, Vilar transformed the huge, three-thousand seat T.N.P. from a garage for others' productions into a center of creation and animation. In addition, the T.N.P.'s repertoire became the source for the popularly priced summer dramatic festivals in Avignon.

Vilar initiated procedures which were later practiced in every playhouse inscribing itself in the popular theater movement: reduced prices (2,000 AF—about $4.50—a season ticket for six plays), no tipping, inexpensive programs and texts of the plays, early hours for working people, and a modest buffet supper for those who had no time to go home to eat before the performance. He and his staff gave lectures to union committees, held discussions with the audience, and distributed questionnaires in order to be informed of their public's preferences. T.N.P.-sponsored buses transported workers to and from the theater; and factories such as Renault reserved two hundred seats a month for their employees.

Vilar accepted and pursued the government's ideal of theater as a public service:

Le T.N.P. est un service public. Il est désormais question . . . d'apporter à la partie la plus vive de la société contemporaine et particulièrement aux femmes et aux enfants de la tâche ingrate et du labeur dur, les charmes d'un plaisir dont ils n'auraient jamais dû, depuis le temps des cathédrales et des mystères, être sevrés (2).

Primarily concerned with familiarizing a popular public with the consecrated classical works of Molière, Corneille, and Shakespeare, he nevertheless devoted a third of his repertoire to contemporary works.

Pleased with the results of Vilar's work, the government took a further step to involve itself in the popular theater movement in 1959 when President De Gaulle appointed André Malraux Minister of Cultural Affairs. For nearly the first time in the history of France, culture no longer came under the domain of the Minister of Education. Defining popular theater, Malraux replaced the concept of popular education with that of cultural action. «Culture for the greatest number» rather than «culture for the workers» became his byword. In an address to the Chambre des Députés Malraux demanded the «right to culture» for every Frenchman:

Il s'agit de faire ce que la IIIe République avait réalisé, dans sa volonté républicaine, pour l'enseignement; il s'agit de faire en sorte que chaque enfant de France puisse avoir droit aux tableaux, au théâtre, au cinéma, etc. comme il a droit à l'alphabet (3).

To insure this right, he inaugurated, in 1961, the program of *maisons de la culture:*

Le lieu de rencontre et de confrontation par excellence, entre la culture
et ceux qui veulent y accéder, entre ceux qui délivrent le message et ceux
qui le reçoivent, entre les artistes et leur public, et tout simplement entre
les hommes entre eux (4).

Financed half by the State and half by the municipalities, the
maisons de la culture were to fill, in the provinces, the cultural
gap which was not met by subsidized dramatic centers and permanent troupes (5).

While the government fostered the notion of theater as a public service and a cultural right, others attempted to realize a
popular theater of political protest. Jean-Paul Sartre, one of the
first to call for a theater which speaks to the masses about their
most serious preoccupations, saw the working class as a truly
revolutionary audience (*Qu'est-ce que la littérature?*). He therefore grafted to his appeal for popular theater the conception of
political consciousness. Sartre led the attack on the «false»
theater of the bourgeoisie which represents passion rather than
action. The bourgeoisie, he criticized, promotes a subjective image of man based on its own values.

His demand for a *littérature engagée* recommends drama
which situates contemporary man in his society:

C'est qu'il n'y a pas de salut individuel: il faut que la Société se change
toute entière; et la fonction du dramaturge reste cette 'purification' dont
parlait Aristote; il nous découvre ce que nous sommes: victimes et com-
plices à la fois. . . . La 'purification' s'appelle aujourd'hui d'un autre nom:
c'est la prise de conscience (6).

The playwright should force each spectator to reexamine his
own and others' social and economic position.

In his own plays, which dominated the post-war French stage
until the early 1950's, Sartre posits the individual's moral responsibility for his own acts while alluding to the responsibilities facing modern France. In *Les Mouches* (1943), he attempts
to liberate the country from the psychological grip of remorse
created by France's World War II defeat; and in *Les Séquestrés
d'Altona* (1959), he challenges the French to assume their guilt
for the torture of Algerians during the Algerian Crisis.

Vilar was getting popular theater off the ground and Sartre

was applauding the death of God and the birth of man (*Le Diable et le Bon Dieu,* 1951) when the theater of the absurd made itself known in experimental left-bank playhouses. Like Sartre, Ionesco and Beckett were conducting postmortems on earlier ethical and metaphysical expectations; but they refused a «way out.» «Understanding» and «responsibility» had no place in their vocabulary. Instead, they integrated their statement of man's absurdity into all the elements of their plays, experimenting with disarticulated language, non-climactic and circular structures, and metaphorical clownish characters in modern dress. Their productions realized the Artaudian notion of *la poésie de l'espace,* freeing internal reality from the need of an external plot and reemphasizing the physical nature of theater. The revolutionary form of their theater, however, while reviving the French stage, proposed no solution to the despair inherent in being human. Theirs was anything but a politicized or popular theater.

By the middle of the 1950's, critics and playwrights began to decry the lack of political consciousness of absurd playwrights. Having «discovered» Brecht in 1954, when the Berlin Ensemble presented *Mother Courage* at the First International Theater Festival, scores of theater professionals were convinced of the importance of the political role of drama: «On peut sans doute attribuer à Brecht—du moins pour une grande part (n'oublions pas *Morts sans sépulture* ou *Nekrassov*) la prise de conscience, en France, d'une certaine fonction sociale du théâtre» (7). They strove to marry the theater's social function to the new forms proposed by the theater of the absurd (8).

Arthur Adamov's reorientation of his theater is significant in this respect. Formerly one of the most successful creators of absurd drama, portraying the impotence of man and the inconsequentiality of life, in 1956 he declared himself a confirmed Brechtian, rejecting the «no man's land éternel, sinistre, consolant, confortable» (9) of absurd theater. Adamov teamed up with Roger Planchon in 1957 at the latter's pioneer popular Théâtre de la Cité in a working-class suburb of Lyon to produce *Paolo Paoli.* The political message of this production clearly illustrates Adamov's transition:

Paolo Paoli marque pour moi, pour mon évolution spirituelle, politique, artistique, une étape très importante. J'ai compris enfin (mieux vaut tard que jamais) qu'une œuvre d'art, et surtout une pièce de théâtre, n'acquiert de réalité que si elle se place dans un contexte social défini, si sa révolution formelle se relie à une révolution interne. Je ne crois plus à cette avant-garde trompeuse qui utilise sans doute des techniques neuves mais oublie que ces techniques neuves sont nulles et non avenues si l'auteur ne se met pas au service d'une idéologie; et naturellement pas de n'importe quelle idéologie, mais par exemple, du marxisme-léninisme—pour nommer les choses par leur nom (10).

Critics termed the Parisian presentation of the play in 1958 the event of the season. *Paolo Paoli* marked the politicization of the avant-garde.

Of the practitioners of the theater of the absurd, Eugène Ionesco alone passionately challenged the importance of political theater. He defended his position in a series of exchanges with theater critic Kenneth Tynan who, in 1958, mounted an anti-absurd campaign in the *Observer.* Ionesco riposted:

Apporter un message aux hommes, vouloir diriger la course du monde, ou le sauver, c'est l'affaire des fondateurs de religions, des moralistes ou des hommes politiques—lesquels, entre parenthèses, s'en tirent plutôt mal, comme nous sommes payés pour le savoir. Un dramaturge se borne à écrire des pièces, dans lesquelles il ne peut qu'offrir un témoignage, non point un message didactique—un témoignage personnel, affectif, de son angoisse et de l'angoisse des autres (11).

Opposing political theater, detesting Brecht and Brechtians, Ionesco refused to condemn social and political systems. Although he attested to the fundamental failure of the modern world, he would not examine the reasons behind it. Ionesco's role in the debate ended when in 1966 his play *La Soif et la faim,* in which he satirizes Brecht, became part of the repertoire of the Comédie Française. With his election to the Académie Française (1970), he promptly parachuted out of the avant-garde.

The reorientation of the avant-garde paralleled the increasing political awareness of the popular theater movement. In addition to Sartre's insights, Brechtian theory especially influenced French theater professionals to infuse popular theater with a political consciousness (12). The review *Théâtre Populaire,* originally conceived to champion the Théâtre National Populaire and the notion of theater as public service, began in 1955 to compare Vilar unfavorably with Brecht, criticizing the former for a lack of political gumption. By 1963, the magazine's editorials suggested that theater should deal with themes of class struggle.

Brecht's insistence on the ethical force of the director and the *mise en scène* did not lie fallow with Vilar, whose productions increasingly aimed at exposing contemporary injustices. In 1959, Vilar chose to stage *Ubu Roi* as a direct protest against De Gaulle's use of personal power during the Algerian War. His frustration with government pressure on the T.N.P.'s operation led to his resignation in 1963.

Other directors of popular theaters, such as Roger Planchon and Marcel Maréchal, prompted by Vilar's practice of theatrical allusion, attempted to «politicize» the classics. They often situated the action and characters of a centuries-old play in an economic or psychological context which has meaning for contemporary times. Planchon's 1964 version of a homosexual *Tartuffe* typified this approach:

Perhaps one could argue that Tartuffe leads Orgon on; but from the point of view of morality—and I am a moralist—the one who acts is the guilty man. Orgon was an important man, a friend of the King. He met Tartuffe in church, brought him home, fed him, clothed him, etc. For the past three hundred years these actions have not been understood. Critics have called Orgon stupid—but a man's actions cannot be explained away that easily. Orgon is not stupid, but profoundly homosexual. It's obvious that he doesn't know it (13).

By choosing to portray Orgon as an unwary homosexual, Planchon challenged three centuries of interpretation. The focus moved from religious hypocrisy to sexual identity, a relevant theme for a twentieth-century audience. Orgon's unconscious homosexuality emphasized the danger of conforming to sex roles. Had he been aware of his own proclivity, Orgon might have been spared Tartuffe's treachery.

Another approach called for the analysis of a play's characters according to the historical and social situation prevailing when the play was written. This kind of analysis rejects both the notion of the eternal nature of man and its corollary—man's inability to change the human condition.

Decentralization took on the dimensions of political protest when various directors, in league with Communist leaders, set up popular theaters in the «red belt,» or working-class districts surrounding Paris. Locating there in the mid 1960's, Gabriel Garran at Aubervilliers, José Valverde at Saint-Denis, Raymond Gerbal at Villejuif, Guy Rétoré in the twentieth *arrondissement* of Paris, and Pierre Debauche at Nanterre worked to involve local populations in the activity of their theaters and to develop a repertoire which dealt with controversial issues facing their particular publics. They refused the role of «keeper of the cultural patrimony» and opted for a theater which stresses class differences.

In the mid 1960's the increasing political awareness of theater professionals and the technical innovations of the theater of the absurd gave birth to a new repertoire of denunciation:

Le premier travail d'un théâtre révolutionnaire n'est pas de dire 'faisons la révolution!' Il ne suffit pas de le dire sur une scène pour qu'elle se fasse. Il faut démontrer les mécanismes de l'aliénation, faire des portraits accusateurs, mettre à jour ce que l'on veut nous cacher, grossir ce que l'on veut nous faire passer pour anodin, hurler lorsqu'on veut nous faire prendre des vessies pour des lanternes (14).

Playwrights such as Armand Gatti, Georges Michel, and Aimé Césaire, while influenced by absurdist techniques, countered the absurd theater's insistence on the futility of existence with the possibility of action. If, in the absurd theater, man is the hopeless stooge of universal laughter, in their politically committed one, he is the unwilling pawn of an economic hierarchy. He possesses both the desire and the means to change his situation; for his dilemma is social and political, not metaphysical.

Armand Gatti, devoting himself to a theater of direct relevance to a working-class public, proclaimed that dramatic action consists in making man pass from the state of victim to that of combattant:

Le bon et le mauvais n'existent pas. Ce qui existe, c'est le contexte et l'effort que fait l'individu pour s'en libérer, se rattacher à un autre contexte ou l'effort qu'il ne fait pas (15).

Believing in theater as an arm for educating the proletariat, he presented each of his early plays to groups of workers in order to test their reactions.

In one of his first plays, *La Vie imaginaire de l'éboueur Auguste Geai,* produced in 1962 at Planchon's Théâtre de la Cité, the protagonist, a garbage collector, reclaims his dignity through his union activities:

Il ne faut quand même pas croire qu'un balayeur et ce qu'il ramasse c'est la même chose; ma vie, elle vaut celle d'un ministre et même celle d'un général (16).

Endearing, paradoxically idealistic and pragmatic, Auguste Geai dies for the «Revolution,» having been beaten by the strike-breakers hired by the Sanitation Department.

Adopting a highly original technique characteristic of all his later productions, Gatti uses parallel and multiple universes to portray the story of Auguste Geai. The stage is divided into seven scenic spaces, five of them representing a different time sequence in Auguste's life. Past, present, and an imaginary future exist simultaneously. Five different actors play Auguste, sometimes speaking one after the other, sometimes in chorus. The action converges on the central platform where the dying Auguste reviews his life.

As in many plays of the absurd, the absence of a chronological sequence eliminates the build-up of suspense and the evolution of the characters. Gatti, therefore, interpolates songs and projections throughout his play, depending on fast transitions and rapid movement to keep the public's attention. The spectator must piece the story together from the information which is provided. Flowing imagistic passages and poetic meditation complement the staccato action and appeal to the spectator's emotions.

Contrary to Gatti's complex portrayal of the human condition, the straightforward structure of the plays of Georges Michel perfectly illustrates his appraisal of human conditioning. Michel concentrates on attacking the mental structures of the *petite bourgeoisie* in order to call attention to «cette immense machination de technocrates, cette 'matérialisation' de l'homme par le conditionnement publicitaire. Ce que Sartre appelle 'l'extéroconditionnement'» (17). Adapting to this end the repetitious and meaningless language and metaphorical characters of the absurd in his 1966 production of *La Promenade du dimanche*, Michel condemns both the blindness of the middle class to its social responsibilities and the commonplace banalities which impair its vision. More specifically, Michel indicts those Frenchmen who chose to ignore the consequences of the Algerian War.

A middle-class family performs the ritualistic Sunday promenade. En route to the movies, «Mother,» «Father,» and «Son» merely shrug their shoulders when «Grandfather» and «Grandmother» are assassinated in the street. Petitioners for civil rights, victims of police brutality, and automated «friends of the family» solicit little interest and less compassion. «Mother» continuously laments that they should have stayed at home as «it's just one of those days»; while «Father» proposes one solution to all the family problems: «Work and save, work and save.» Only «Son» occasionally dares look beyond the platitudes of his parents. At the end of the play, when he too becomes the victim of an unseen gunman, his parents finally face the horrifying consequences of their indifference.

Unlike Michel, who specializes in blackly satirical portraits, Aimé Césaire invests his political reflections with lyrical poetry. Combining the scope of Elizabethan drama with elements of African ritual, *La Tragédie du Roi Christophe*, Césaire's first produced play (1964), embodies both a warning to leaders of emerging African nations and a vision of the grandeur such nations might achieve.

With this play, Césaire, aided by the director Jean-Marie Serreau, established the French-language theater of black consciousness. King Christophe, nineteenth-century revolutionary and ruler of the northern province of Haiti, is the pivotal figure in Césaire's theater of *la négritude*. Although defeated by the treachery of his followers and the extravagance of his own demands, he leaves a heritage of black pride and energy:

Il est temps de mettre à la raison ces nègres qui croient que la Révolution ça consiste à prendre la place des Blancs et continuer, en lieu et place, je veux dire sur le dos des nègres, à faire le Blanc (18).

His actions denounce and reveal the anguish in blackness, while illustrating to the rest of the world the problems of former colonies striving for cultural and economic independence.

Césaire explains this latter aspect of the play:

Le drame haïtien illustre à la perfection la tragédie de l'exercice du pouvoir dans les Etats dont l'accession à l'indépendance est récente. . . . Christophe se débat dans une solitude effarante, comme . . . Senghor ou Modibo Keita, mais il dispose de moyens d'actions bien inférieurs à ceux des dirigeants politiques de l'Afrique noire contemporaine (19).

The playwright would have old European nations take heed to listen to future Christophes and new African states take caution to escape the original Christophe's fate.

Whether partaking in the Third World Theater movement spearheaded by Césaire and Serreau, irreverently celebrating the death of accepted values like Michel, or bulldozing through social and economic barriers like Gatti, the playwrights of the theater of denunciation of the 1960's all desired to raise the consciousness of their spectators (20). However, with the exception of Jean Genet, none of them advocated the total destruction of existing society, nor did they foster real change in the structure of the theatrical institution. Despite the Marxist sympathies of many of these authors, they did not pit one social class against another. They were chiefly interested in getting all men to see how and why they were in a specific social or economic situation.

By 1968, protest theater, plays of denunciation, and politicized stagings composed the major part of theatrical productions in France. Not only private theaters but also government-subsidized popular ones produced the work of Gatti, Michel, Césaire, and playwrights with similar political concepts. Unfortunately these productions reached mainly middle-class audiences. By the mid 1960's attempts to bring the worker to the theater had greatly decreased (21). Playwrights subscribing to a political theater for a popular public found themselves producing their plays in theaters no longer popular. The weight of government administration had begun to crush the popular theater movement, which concerned itself less and less with the interaction of public and repertoire and more and more with financial questions:

On peut craindre en particulier que le théâtre soit sacrifié à une 'culturo-manie,' il se préoccupe davantage d'un bon fonctionnement administratif d'organismes de production culturelle que d'une création artistique libre et indépendante (22).

Despite the inventiveness of a few theater professionals, a general malaise, echoed in society at large, had settled over popular and political theater alike. When the events of May demanded a reconsideration of popular and political theater in France, theater professionals were at last prepared to come to grips with the effects of Marxism on theatrical activity.

Chapter III

MAY '68 AND THE THEATER

Tout le monde sait qu'au rêve humaniste de l'après-guerre a succédé un autre temps, une autre époque, et que sur les balbutiements et les tentatives des années 60 est passé Mai 68; alors, s'est ouverte une période radicalement différente, dont certains entrevoient avec peine ce qu'elle sera mais dont tous savent que l'exercice du théâtre—entre autres—y sera radicalement changé.

Patrice Chéreau, «Comment faire du théâtre populaire en 1972,» *Le Monde*, 20 July 1972, p. 11.

Les Evénements de Mai, just as *la Révolution, la Commune*, and *la Résistance* have entered the realm of popular French mythology, constituting the latest criteria for marking change. In qualifying their commentaries with *avant Mai* or *depuis Mai*, French social and esthetic critics, professional or non-professional, bear witness to the force with which one month of spontaneous demonstrations and economic chaos imposed itself on the national consciousness. However, if the events of May '68 implanted themselves firmly in the French mind, they had little effect upon the economic and political situation being contested.

The Sorbonne students who initiated the demonstrations, both in solidarity with their more provocative Nanterre colleagues and in protest against the French university's conservative policies, found themselves subjected in October 1969 to a more inadequate and confused system than the previous year's muddle. The workers, whose original sympathy for the student movement was skillfully mobilized by their unions into a general strike for higher wages and better working conditions, discovered that the increased living costs of the post-May period outweighed their negotiated benefits. Finally, the parliamentary opposition, despite the Gaullist government's mishandling of the crisis, lost more than half of its seats in the June 1968 elections. As theater critic Bernard Dort incisively comments, «En mai 1968, partisans de la fête et partisans de l'action, se rencontrèrent un moment dans l'illusion lyrique d'une révolution qui serait aussi pur théâtre» (1). French society turned itself into a spectacle, but was impotent to alter its prevailing economic and political structures.

Why, then, despite the failure of its diverse goals, does the evocation of May '68 not only produce nostalgia but also stimulate hope? Perhaps because, as implied in Dort's analysis and as interpreted by Michel Butor, the individual who gave himself up to the enthusiasm of May and to its commitment to change very often discovered both the liberating force of participatory drama and his own creative personality. As Butor puts it, «Chaque écaille de ce dragon [the May movement] est un livre qui reprend vie» (2). Creative activity, extending from a hundred specialized study groups to the revolutionary *ateliers* of l'Ecole des Beaux-Arts, eclipsed routine preoccupations, bestowing a festive ambiance upon the «Revolution.» The upheaval of conventions and habits invited and even required freeing oneself from an unquestioned acceptance of society. People were forced to rethink their political position and their personal ambitions, to discover what annoyed or embittered them and to posit a remedy. The streets became open forums in which heteroclite groups discussed their grievances without fear of official repression. When on May 13 the student demonstrators occupied the Sorbonne and opened it to continuous debate and revolutionary planning committees, imagination imposed itself as the only legitimate ruler.

For a certain number of men and women touched by the May events, those for whom creativity is a constant preoccupation and not merely the momentary gift of a social upheaval, May yielded more than hope. Swept into the creative chaos of May as much by their esthetic affinity as by their political views, artists found their work emerging as one of the focal points of protest.

In early spring 1968, committees on creativity, formed at the Université de Paris at Nanterre under the aegis of the March 22 Movement, attacked capitalist culture (3). These committees determined that culture, like the university, was a bourgeois weapon used to manipulate and menace the working class. If revolutionary protest did not inform cultural activities, then these activities should be destroyed. During the May strikes, a group of Sorbonne students known as the Comité d'Agitation Culturelle launched discussions on similar themes. The Comité Révolutionnaire d'Action Culturelle (aptly abbreviated as C.R.A.C.), also from the Sorbonne, embodied its opinion on the necessity of the revolutionary role of the artist in a series of poems such as the following:

Je persiste à penser
Que la place d'un poète en ce moment
Est dans la rue
Que vous devez prendre d'assaut
Les tours d'ivoire Les raser
Proclamer
L'Etat d'urgence
Quand je me laisse aller
A pleurnicher sur ma misère
Si cette misère n'est pas aussi
La tienne
Lecteur
Frappe-moi fort
Qu'il n'y ait plus
De poésie absente (4).

Another group, the Comité d'Action Révolutionnaire (5), which masterminded the Odéon occupation during the night of

May 15-16, once again defined art as an elitist industry with capitalist designs: «Le théâtre, le cinéma, la peinture, la littérature, etc. . . . sont devenus des industries accaparées par une élite dans un but d'aliénation et de mercantilisme» (6).

Professional artists themselves registered complaints relating specifically to their art form. Writers founded the Union des Ecrivains to determine the goal of the writer in society and establish a method of ending his victimization in the production-consumption cycle. Of the thirty painters who withdrew their works from the Salon de Mai in protest against consumer society, several, including Matta, re-exhibited in striking factories. Illustrators sold posters in the Sorbonne for the benefit of imprisoned students. And Claude Lelouch, Alain Resnais, and Milos Forman refused to participate in the Cannes film festival on the grounds of its apolitical orientation.

Of all the artists touched by the May explosion, the actors, directors, and technicians of France's theaters experienced the most severe shock. Perhaps this was because of the vulnerable situation of the theater, already shaken by a decade of self-analysis, or perhaps the theater's generic need to interact with a contemporary public prompted its immediate and somewhat convulsive response. In any case, by designating the Odéon as the symbol of bourgeois and Gaullist culture, the invading *enragés* of the Sorbonne placed the theater at the center of protest.

The theatrical season of 1967-1968 produced no portents of the May '68 crisis as accurate as Jean-Luc Godard's film *La Chinoise*. However, a number of plays prophesied a society about to explode. As Bertrand Poirot-Delpech, critic for *Le Monde*, noted, «Cette saison recèle . . . tous les signes avant-coureurs d'une rupture brutale» (7). Furthermore, the choice of the 1967-1968 repertoire indicated the end of one theatrical era and the advent of another. The revival of some of the major productions of the theater of the absurd paradoxically signaled its «swan song.» A series of plays brutally satirizing society and demanding action countered the resignation in absurdist works. In the same vein, the French named as the major discoveries of the 1968 International Theater Festival at Nancy the American

Bread and Puppet Theater, an agit-prop group using street-theater techniques, and El Teatro Oficino, a radical troupe from Brazil.

Denunciation was indeed the most obvious and successful motif of the plays of 1967-1968. They criticized precisely those attitudes and institutions under fire in May. Philippe Adrien in *La Baye* and Jean-Claude Grumberg in *Demain, une fenêtre sur rue*, for example, examined the heedlessness of the bourgeoisie which promotes its own destruction. The youngest sons of the Louis Family and the Jean Family in *La Baye* incarnate the promise of revolt against their parents' vulgar stupidity; and Huguette, the exalted daughter of Grumberg's Duplantin family, sides with *ceux-d'en-bas* in their guerilla warfare against the Establishment, of which her father is an exemplary member.

The principal objective of both these plays, to satirize the ideas and conduct of the upper middle class, is successfully met by Adrien's Ionesco-like word plays and by Grumberg's telling analysis of a family under siege. While Adrien's characters talk around each other, Grumberg's people talk at each other, clinging to their bourgeois truisms despite the approaching revolutionaries. Both plays expose the omnipresent *mauvaise foi* in liberal bourgeois philosophy. M. Duplantin's speech, as he looks out over the street battle, typifies his hypocritical posture:

Mais c'est réellement ici, de cette fenêtre, que j'ai senti pour la première fois le peu d'importance de la vie humaine. . . . Oui, en fait, seul comptent l'équilibre, la stabilité, les structures (8)!

His insistence on law and order over understanding seems prophetic in light of the end of the May events. However, in M. Duplantin's case, law and order are precluded by an off-target bomb which kills his entire family.

No such end disturbs the philosophical drivel of the characters in René Ehni's play *Que ferez-vous en novembre?* His tired intellectuals, disgusted with themselves and nostalgic for the leftist demonstrations of yesteryear, have only cynicism for tomorrow:

Ah ces hommes de gauche. Ils sont polis, bien élevés, ils ont lu Marx dans tous les sens et Lénine a dit Trotsky a dit Engels a dit, ils ne battent pas leur femme, ils s'écartent dans l'escalier pour laisser passer la bonne espagnole, ils ne traumatisent pas les enfants, ils n'élèvent jamais la voix, ils signent, ils marchent, ils protestent. Mais ils ne font pas la révolution (9).

Their one achievement, doubtlessly inspired by Saint-Exupéry, is to have retrieved a young Alsatian painter, Urs (an obvious slur on the U.S.S.R.), from the working class which bore him:

On a eu toutes les peines du monde à le convaincre, lui et son papa, qu'il fallait laisser tomber l'usine pour l'Art. Tous trois nous avons suppléé à la carence de l'Etat bourgeois qui ne fait rien pour les petits Mozart du peuple et nous l'avons fait monter, Mozart, vers l'Art et vers Paris, la capitale (10).

If Urs proclaims the necessity of a revolution and the establishment of a worker's culture, he is, nonetheless, as willingly impotent to act as his mentors. Totally assimilated into the bourgeoisie, he even foregoes his painting to gad about Europe with an iron magnate's daughter. Ehni's pessimism, which renders his satire barely palatable, challenged intellectuals in May. Most refused to accept their political futility and sought to align their action with their words.

In *Les Treize Soleils de la rue St.-Blaise*, Armand Gatti advances the argument of *récupération* later heard in May study groups. While some of his working-class characters aspire to the culture of the bourgeoisie, others feel the need to invent a new culture grounded in their own experience. One accuses his night-school teacher of fostering a culture of dead revolutions:

Vous représentez la culture (une certaine culture qui consiste à rechauffer les fêtes mortes de l'esprit), les grandes révolutions de l'esprit, désamorcées sans le contexte qui leur donnait leur violence et leur insécurité—les grandes révolutions enfin confortables, habitables, avec robinets, pour eau chaude et eau froide, réfrigérateur et air conditionné (11).

Also foreseen in this play are the contradictions which racked the May revolutionary committees. The commissions which Gatti's characters form in order to discuss ways of improving their situation are totally disunited on the questions of women's liberation, class-consciousness, and revolutionary action. For all

his premonitory vision, Gatti was taken by surprise when the
May events erupted, perhaps because he, like the other playwrights mentioned, and despite their sensitivity to the collective
consciousness, only foresaw May as fiction.

Of all the plays of the 1967-1968 season, *Les Héritiers,* a collective creation by the university troupe the Aquarium, was the
most directly connected with the events of May '68. Adapted
from a sociological study by Bourdieu and Passeron (*Les Héritiers: Les Etudiants et la culture,* Paris: Minuit, 1964) on the
inequalities of educational opportunity, the play depicts a number of student problems and, in particular, the contrasting situation of two students, Armand I (from a working-class family)
and his double, Armand II (from a bourgeois family), as they
prepare for a major examination. Armand II, assured, sophisti-
cated, encouraged by his family and a chorus of other bourgeois
heirs, succeeds not by *savoir* but by *savoir-faire,* while Armand
I, anguished, plodding, and solitary, fails. The moral of the
story is clear: «Hors de l'Ecole point de salut / L'Ecole élit les
élus» (12).

The theme of educational discrimination based on class preoccupied the members of the Aquarium as well as the student
protestors of May. The troupe's goal—to expose university problems to a student public—was fully realized in May during the
demonstrations when the play was specially performed in the
courtyard of l'Ecole des Beaux-Arts. A passionate debate followed the performance with actors and audience engaged in a
general critique of the university.

So that *Les Héritiers* might be as relevant as possible to the
changing social crisis, the Aquarium continued to modify it
during May, finally switching its emphasis from inequality to
repression. The original criticism of middle-class student protestors who boycott exams (thereby compromising the working-
class student's chance of success) was eliminated. In the final
version of the play, the examination administrator, wearing a
C.R.S. hat (13) and carrying a nightstick, bullies all the students
into taking their exams, a premonition of what eventually did
happen, albeit a bit more subtly, the following autumn.

The willingness with which the Aquarium, a university elite, sabotaged its privileged position crowned the growing propensity in the 1960's to disparage the bourgeoisie and, with it, the capitalist system. In May 1968 dissatisfaction with this system, and all institutions related to it, became too great to be encompassed in words. Revolution escaped a fictional framework.

When the May crisis was fully underway, traditional theater of text, despite its protest value, was no longer possible. Criticism took to the streets. People did not want to go to the theater to watch society being denounced when they could partake in the denunciation themselves. Only *Les Héritiers*, because of its formal flexibility, continued to be performed during the course of the month.

With theaters abandoned, playwrights, actors, and directors did not hesitate long before taking part in the street spectacle outside. Spurred on by the May 15 occupation of the Odéon, theater professionals responded to the crisis both through a re-examination of their own needs and role in society and by a type of dramatic production best suited to the revolutionary movement.

The theatrical unions were the first to react officially. In solidarity with the student movement, the most important union conglomerate, the Confédération Générale du Travail (C.G.T.), of which several theatrical unions are members, called a general strike on Monday, May 13. Five days later, a meeting of twelve hundred actors and technicians of the Syndicat Français des Acteurs (S.F.A.) at the Théâtre National Populaire resulted in the May 21 summons for an unlimited work-stoppage. By May 22, all the national and private theaters, with the exception of the Gymnase, had closed (14). In addition, the workers of the Opéra Comique, technicians of the Théâtre National Populaire and the Théâtre de l'Ést Parisien occupied their buildings, while diverse committees of actors, technicians, students, and local residents at Bourges, Grenoble, Aix-en-Provence, and Villejuif began the occupations of the provincial popular theaters and *maisons de la culture*. Under union auspices, commissions began to study means of ameliorating working conditions and theater management.

The response to the union activities reflects the divergent tendencies of the «Revolution» itself. For soon after the S.F.A. called the unlimited strike, a group of actors and directors, notably Alain Delon, Raymond Gérôme, and Jacques Dacqmine (all Gaullists), refused the order and broke away to form their own professional union, stating:

Nous sommes persuadés, que la grève illimitée du spectacle ne servira en rien les intérêts professionels des manifestants, les activités des spectacles n'étant pas vitales à la vie de la nation (15).

While Delon and friends moved to the right, abjuring all tactics of political pressure, another one hundred and fifty actors leaned to the left, dissolving their ties with the S.F.A. because of its refusal, under C.G.T. direction, to continue supporting the students. By the end of May, their meetings multiplying, theater professionals had to opt for corporate reformism or revolutionary activism. On the one hand, groups like the Syndicat National des Metteurs en Scène Dramatiques, Lyriques et Choréographiques proposed concrete changes in theater administration and price control; on the other, independent gatherings of actors and directors, such as one including Roger Blin, Delphine Seyrig, and members of the Institut d'Etudes Théâtrales, created committees supporting political street theater rather than internal reform. Furthermore, some professionals, particularly those involved in the Odéon takeover, refused theatrical activity entirely, preferring political militancy:

En ce qui concerne les théâtres, la moindre activité corporative, le moindre spectacle organisé *intra-muros*, le moindre relâchement de l'agitation révolutionnaire serait une trahison de l'élan qui s'est révélé sur les barricades et qui doit à tout prix non pas diminuer mais augmenter en puissance (16).

The dichotomy of political action and theatrical reform continued to wreak havoc in the institution even after the S.F.A. terminated the strike on June 4 in response to negotiations with the government. Most private theaters reopened by June 10. However, C.R.A.C., the Sorbonne revolutionary committee for cultural action, entered several of them in opposition, interrupting the performances and denouncing the theater's complicity with those in power. It complained, «Les C.R.S. frappent les trois coups, le théâtre ouvre» (17). Long after the Odéon's one hundred and thirty-seven occupants were evacuated on June 14, the discord in the theater community persisted. The events of May 1968 had forced actors, directors, and playwrights to take a hard look at their professions, and many of them would not be content with mere material concessions. They demanded a change in theatrical orientation as well.

Among those seeking to reorient the theater was a group of forty-two directors of the *maisons de la culture* and other popular theaters. The events of May encouraged them to do something about the stagnation that had beset the popular theater movement. Invited by Roger Planchon, they met at the end of May in his Villeurbanne theater to draw up a declaration of the «rights of the public and duties of the producers.» They stated that the month's events had brutally awakened them to the cultural gaps between different socio-economic groups, and they invented the term *non-public* to designate those people normally outside the theater's reach:

Une immensité humaine composée de tous ceux qui n'ont encore aucun accès ni aucune chance d'accéder prochainement au phénomène culturel sous les formes qu'il persiste à revêtir dans la presque totalité des cas (18).

Their goal, and indeed the justification of their public existence, would be to reach this *non-public*, thus destroying its cultural isolation.

Up to this point, the declaration did not essentially modify the existing philosophy behind popular theater. However, the Villeurbanne committee went on to explain the means by which it hoped to achieve this goal, and through its explanation it developed a new theory of *action culturelle*. Previously, this term, which underlay the founding of the *maisons de la culture*, meant providing an easy access to the cultural heritage. To the men gathered at Villeurbanne, *action culturelle* became, however, a way of helping the *non-public* situate itself in its social and historical context—that is, to politicize itself:

C'est pourquoi tout effort d'ordre culturel ne pourra plus que nous apparaître vain aussi longtemps qu'il ne se proposera pas expressément d'être une entreprise de politisation: c'est-à-dire d'inventer sans relâche, à l'inten-

tion de ce 'non-public,' des occasions de se politiser, de se choisir libre-
ment, par-delà le sentiment d'impuissance et d'absurdité que ne cesse de
susciter en lui un système social où les hommes ne sont pratiquement jamais en mesure d'inventer *ensemble* leur propre humanité (19).

Cultural action must henceforth modify contemporary relation-
ships between men, develop their class-consciousness and self-
determination.

Rather than choosing between theater and politics the Villeurbanne declaration attempted to reconcile the two by making
theater the means to achieve political consciousness. Although it
was Brechtian in inspiration, any attempt to see a clearly defined
Marxist philosophy behind it can only bog down in the declaration's ambiguous phrasing. Capitalism as such is not condemned
nor is the bourgeoisie rendered evil. The closest thing to a call to
revolution is the desire to help men «à inventer *ensemble* leur
propre humanité.»

This declaration was, then, criticized by those who thought
its signers did not go far enough in their political commitment.
José Valverde, the director of the Théâtre Gérard Philip at St.-
Denis and a member of the Communist Party, stated his position bluntly:

Je le dis brutalement . . . ce qui m'a frappé à Villeurbanne mais frappé
comme le jour en sortant de 24 heures d'obscurité, c'est le côté analpha-
bète politiquement de tous mes collègues. . . . Ils ne savent rien, rien, rien
de la vie politique française, ces directeurs de théâtre. Ils sortent péremp-
toirement des âneries qui sont éculées depuis un siècle (20).

But the declaration was also censured by those who found its
missionary attitude reprehensible. In any case, the Villeurbanne
Committee's appeal to reorient the theater had a more fertile aftermath than any of the concrete demands (such as an increase
in the cultural affairs allocations and the creation of a European
Common Market of spectacles) put to the government by union
representatives.

While the directors of the *maisons de la culture* and popular
theaters were defining new theatrical policies at Villeurbanne,
their co-workers remaining in the theaters decided to reach the
non-public—out of work, on strike, and thus accessible. Their

activity comprised the major part of what can be termed the «theater of May.» From approximately May 20 to June 10, suburban «red-belt» theaters, popular provincial theater groups, and various small troupes joined the general strike movement under the guise of a *grève active,* which meant stopping their scheduled activity in order to produce plays, films, cabaret shows, and poetry montages in the occupied factories.

Although their own initiative permitted troupes such as that of the Théâtre de la Commune d'Aubervilliers to enter these factories, several troupes, those of Gennevilliers and St.-Denis in particular, had to appeal to the Communist organization «Travail et Culture,» an affiliate of the C.G.T., to arrange their performances. Often, however, the strikers themselves, through the cultural committees of their unions, requested theatrical entertainment, inviting such troupes as the Théâtre de l'Est Parisien and the Théâtre du Soleil. Regardless of how the various troupes became involved, their reasons for doing so were generally similar: to keep the strike going by helping the strikers surmount their boredom; to question and discuss problems of the theatrical profession with the workers, thus rendering theater less exotic; and to provide a means of political information. Without question, all of the troupes entering the factories wanted to entertain and therefore included many singers, variety stars, and commercial films in their programming. However, their primary purpose was to stimulate debate about the immediate political crisis.

Provoking debate was also the major concern of the only other type of ongoing theater in May: street theater. Of the street theater groups which sprang to life during the month, one in particular, L'Action Culturelle, valued the post-performance discussion with the audience more than the play itself: «Le genre d'essais auxquels nous nous sommes livrés n'a de valeur que dans ce qui le précède ou le suit et repose sur l'éphémère» (21). Committed to theater only as a means of political action, not an end in itself, it wanted to agitate, not to entertain. L'Action Culturelle therefore put on a series of two to three-minute vignettes in the *quartier* Mouffetard which were designed to elicit immediate responses and active participation from the assembled pedestrians.

Whether in the factories or in the street, the theater of May had to adapt itself to certain performance limitations as well as to the political furor of the moment. Whenever possible, the troupes performing in the factories used a suitable play from their repertoire. In most cases, however, the length, complexity, or subject of their past plays made this impossible. To deal with this situation, teams of writers, technicians, and actors either pieced together dramatic montages or established basic improvisational patterns. Sometimes workers themselves participated in the creation of a montage or suggested themes for improvisations before the performance. They also helped the actors set up their equipment and, if necessary, construct the stage.

Even more restricted in its use of props and number of actors, street theater limited itself to short vignettes of only a few minutes' duration. The text for one of these, if a text existed, was explicit, usually building swiftly up to a climax, often repetitive, and reinforced by direct visual imagery. Like the theater seen in the factories, street theater, flexible and mobile, could be performed wherever there was an available audience.

Of the four basic forms of the theater of May (the written text with a well-defined structure and fairly long duration, the improvisation, the montage, and the short, concise sketch), the montage was by far the most common, with the traditional text the rarest. The two major concerns of the theater of May were the nature of theater and political protest. However, political protest informed the majority of the theater pieces of the period.

An analysis of three representative productions will illustrate more specifically the theater of May: *The Kitchen*, a play by Arnold Wesker, translated and performed by the Théâtre du Soleil; *Le Spondegaulanthrope*, a montage by Henri Delmas, Christiane Lücke, and Catherine Monnot, produced by the Théâtre de la Commune d'Aubervilliers; and *La Promenade de M. Dimanche*, a vignette by the street theater troupe, L'Action Culturelle.

The Kitchen, the only established play of the three, received great critical acclaim and public attention when first performed in the 1966-1967 theatrical season. Ariane Mnouchkine and the

Théâtre du Soleil had revived it for their 1968 spring tour when the May strikes began. For their twenty or so performances in occupied factories, they made almost no changes in the play's *mise en scène,* paralyzed factories providing excellent settings for the mechanized existence of the kitchen workers portrayed in the text. The equation *cuisine* = *usine* appeared more than obvious to the working-class audience, whose sensitivity had naturally been heightened by the precise circumstances under which it saw the play:

Et cela sautait aux yeux que ce n'était plus seulement intellectuellement, comme dans une salle de spectacle, que les spectateurs recevaient le texte; ils étaient de plein-pied avec ces trente hommes et femmes se débattant dans leur cuisine (22).

For them, the microcosmic vision became a well-defined and appropriate comment on their actual situation, much as *Waiting for Godot* revealed itself to the prisoners of San Quentin when performed there in 1957. When one of the main characters, the restaurant owner, angrily exploded at the play's end, oblivious to his employees' aspirations and his own cupidity, the strikers reacted as though they themselves had been insulted. To this character's question, «What more do you need?», they replied in excited debates after the performance, finding the apolitical bent of the kitchen staff both foolish and disheartening. At another time and with different spectators such a reaction would not have occurred. More than one character of *The Kitchen* is plagued by moral ambiguities; and an audience could easily focus its attention on the psychological disintegration of the protagonist Peter, rather than on the opposition management-workers. Nevertheless, the concurrence of a predisposed audience and the potential polemical element in the play succeeded in transforming the play's thrust from reflection to agitation.

The polemical element in the Aubervilliers production of *Le Spondegaulanthrophe,* a half-hour montage, is evident from the moment the spondegaulanthrope, a monstrous caricature of General De Gaulle, makes his stage entrance. The workers who gathered in factory courtyards to watch the beast dance to the Ubu overture and hear him emit obscenities could not mistake the target of the satire. The giant marionette extolls his divinity through his mouthpiece, the *gaulleur,* who then responds evasively to questions from a facetious interviewer. The *gaulleur*'s bombastic statements about France's economy, reform programs, and foreign policy were taken from actual speeches by the President of the Republic. In the montage his statements are made to appear completely vacuous. For example, when asked, «Que penses-tu de la réduction des impôts?» the *gaulleur* replies, «Vive le Québec libre!» (23). Not only is De Gaulle satirized through the content of his own speeches and by his farcical appearance, but a chorus of his more celebrated supporters, designated by hand-held painted caricatures, intervenes several times to back up his statements with nonsense verse, acerbic puns, and spirited word-play. They proclaim as one of the «Ten Commandments» of his political legitimacy, «Etre fort de constitution et en constitution de ne pas être prisonnier de la constitution et de ne pas se constituer prisonnier.»

A tape recording of gongs, cymbals, drums, chants from the May demonstration, and the «Internationale» punctuates and indirectly comments on the interview. The frivolity and burlesque ambiance abruptly turn to a menace at the end, however, when the *gaulleur* hysterically screams «Je ne partirai pas.» As the spondegaulanthrope turns into a black, foreboding monolith, the interviewer approaches the spectators, appealing to them to unite against this perverse force:

> Le temps des illusions n'est pas mort
> ouvrez les yeux . . .
> tout doit être arraché
> mais ce n'est qu'ensemble, rien qu'ensemble
> que nous déboiserons le chemin.

This pattern of exposure followed by agitation is basic to the political montages of the period. The fast-paced visual metaphors and verbal clowning give way at the end to direct address to the audience, inciting it to action and debate, sometimes inviting the audience to join in a snake dance symbolizing solidarity.

A similar design is found in the vignettes of the street theater group L'Action Culturelle, although their limited performance span does not permit the same treatment of the target. The two to three-minute sketches concentrate on one controversial topic such as repression, rather than take on the entire government. A discussion of *La Promenade de M. Dimanche* (inspired by George Michel's *La Promenade du dimanche*) explains how the street sketch provokes an angry reaction. This sketch was performed in the streets in June 1968 at the time of the legislative elections. It deals, appropriately, with voter psychology. While M. Dimanche, the traditionally stolid secure bourgeois, is taking a walk, several actors placed among the crowd cry out in turn to him: «Où allez-vous Monsieur Dimanche?» (24). This question is always followed by a different point of information as to the actual situation in France, such as «L'Université est envahie par les C.R.S.» M. Dimanche, still walking, habitually avoids the questions and counters the information with a disarming nonchalance, having managed to ignore or overcome all of the problems presented by the actors. This pattern continues, with each succeeding item of information growing more atrocious, thus rendering M. Dimanche's imperturbability more heinous. When, at the climax, all the interrogators demand in one voice his destination, he finally becomes annoyed and answers the question: «Mais enfin réfléchissez. Laissez-moi passer. Je vais *voter*!» The spectators have no doubt as to whom he will vote for. However, having just been bombarded with all the reasons why they should not do the same, they can only criticize his choice in the ensuing debate.

If the «theater of May» was successful in propagating both information and agitation, it had to do so most often at the expense of durability, not only of the individual works but also of the interest it awakened in people who had never before been to the theater. Bernard Sobel notes that the strikers who saw his production of Brecht's *L'Exception et la règle* identified so entirely with the conflict in the play that they could not accept their intense experience as a theatrical one:

Le paradoxe est que cette pièce collait tellement aux événements de Mai que les spectateurs des usines ont demandé quand nous reviendrions pour faire du théâtre! Parce que la pièce leur semblait tellement utile, correspondait tellement à leurs problèmes—et elle a permis des débats politiques très approfondis—que pour eux, ce n'était pas du théâtre. Pour eux le théâtre est par essence quelque chose d'inutile, un objet de luxe (25).

For them, theater remained a mysterious and elusive domain. Indeed, other such encounters with the working-class public proved ephemeral. Its original enthusiasm waned when actors returned to legitimate stages the following autumn.

A case can be made for the positive aspects of the «theater of May.» It did successfully aid the revolutionary impetus by supporting the strikers as well as providing a catalyst for political debate. And it reached a new public, one on which popular theater had long concentrated but never quite reached. Moreover, it provided for those directors and actors who were involved in it a privileged moment of experimentation and freedom.

In the immediate aftermath of the May events, discouraged by the return to the status quo, theater professionals looked upon the possibilities of effecting the integration of theater and politics with skepticism and sometimes anger. At the summer 1968 theater festival in Avignon, about one hundred actors and students, with members of C.R.A.C. and l'Action Culturelle, violently contested the festival's conservative function. Despite the official Avignon forum on «Theater and Society,» newly established by its director, Jean Vilar, protestors chose to hold their discussions in the streets. Not content to decry the capitalist orientation of the festival, they demonstrated when the play La Paillasse aux seins nus was forbidden, disrupted performances of the Béjart Ballet, and vociferously supported the Living Theater when it was expelled for disturbing public order.

The protestors did not succeed in destroying the festival. They did, however, demonstrate that theater is not neutral but an arm of the establishment as well as of the revolution. One of the street skits, La Culture, performed at the festival by l'Action Culturelle, satirized the manner in which the events of May became institutionalized—and thus deprived of their revolutionary potential. Two of the characters from the skit promote a new play on «May»:

Orientateur culturel:
Grace à notre nouvelle association de spectateurs du théâtre «Bêta» vous allez pouvoir assister à la nouvelle pièce de théâtre révolutionnaire, par la Troupe Révolutionnaire subventionnée par le Ministre des Affaires Culturelles. Cette pièce s'intitule «Mai, mai, mai, y a pas de Mai.»
Agent de publicité:
Elle est éditée chez Gallimard et vendue dans le commerce au prix de 17,50 Frs. . . . Réduction de 15% aux anciens combattants des barricades sur présentation de leurs cicatrices (26).

Their dialogue illustrates how the establishment controls revolutionary energy by encapsulating and marketing it.

While Avignon demonstrators protested that a theater run by and for the ruling class is an instrument of political repression, Parisian playwrights asked themselves if there were *any* theater which might serve a revolution. Dimitri Dimitriadis' *Le Prix de la révolte au marché noir* typifies the disillusionment which dominated the 1968-1969 repertoire. In Dimitriadis' play, performed in the fall of 1968 by the dramatic company of Patrice Chéreau, a university troupe is portrayed in deep discussion over what it can do to censure the country's dictators. While an anti-government student demonstration takes place in the street, the tyrannical King and Queen themselves unexpectedly arrive at the theater and demand to participate in the troupe's rehearsal. By assuming the parts of the fictional rulers in the troupe's new play, the King and Queen masterfully co-opt the play's protest value. Formerly its target, they become its interpreters, thoroughly confusing illusion and reality. Only when the outside demonstrators invade the theater at the end of the play does the Queen's seductive performance fail. Not political theater, but rather political activism succeeds in toppling her regime.

Of course, not all the plays written under the impetus of May denigrate the theater's revolutionary potential. Some, like *Mai '68 en France* by Jean Thibaudeau, merely recount the May events in a montage. Others, like Arrabal's *L'Imagination-Révolution ou l'Aurore rouge et noire*, transform May into a lyrical theatrical game. The best play written on the crisis, Jean Thénevin's *Octobre à Angoulême*, both satirizes and laments the failure of the May revolt, comparing its aftermath with the outcome of the Russian Revolution.

Because the events of May had so profoundly shaken the theater community, the turmoil at Avignon and the prevailing confusion of theater professionals in the 1968-1969 theatrical season were not unexpected. In fact, this discord provided an extremely fertile opportunity for examining the theater. The best productions of 1968-1969 *were* «theater on theater.»

In the post-May period, playwrights, actors, and directors of subsidized popular theater began to see more clearly their limitations and possibilities; this was especially true of Jo Tréhard of the *maison de la culture* of Caen, and Jean-Louis Barrault, both of whom lost the government's support and consequently their jobs because of their May activity. For many, the concept of the *maison de la culture* had failed to provide the kind of popular theater defined in the Villeurbanne doctrine. Moreover, when the Minister of Culture discontinued meeting with the Villeurbanne Committee, rejecting its idea of *action culturelle* and creating a special governmental service for traditional cultural action, it became clear that revolutionary theater had to find another base. The government's censure of Gatti's play *La Passion du Général Franco,* originally scheduled for winter 1969 at the T.N.P., and the cut in allocations to various *maisons de la culture,* confirmed this need.

In late 1969, there emerged a new political theater. Combining the goals of popular and political theater with formal experimentation, at least twenty young troupes radicalized or created by the May movement made themselves known in Paris and, especially, the provinces. Analyzing this post-May theater in *Le Monde,* Bertrand Poirot-Delpech comments:

Branle-bas dans tous les arts du spectacle: tandis que le grand public continue à consommer du divertissement et de la beauté réputés apolitiques, la presque totalité des artistes de moins de 30 ans brûlent de s'identifier aux exclus de la culture et de saper en leur nom la société en place (27).

Small, financially handicapped, these troupes opted unreservedly for a leftist, often Marxist-oriented theater. Their commitment impelled many of them to shatter their bondage to the established social and theatrical system. All of them were determined to involve the public in their activities. Most willingly diminished the importance of the individual writer in order to create collectively works directly related to their political interests. Actors and directors found their own roles changing and their theatrical work more integrated with their lives.

Chapter IV

LE THEATRE DU SOLEIL:
THEATER AS REVOLUTION, REVOLUTION AS THEATER

> Les rapports du politique et du théâtral sont loins d'être simples. Sauf à faire des spectacles dans la rue, à des fins de propagande et d'action immédiate (on sait à quels obstacles on se heurte alors), le théâtre doit, pour remplir sa mission politique, aussi se mettre en question lui-même. C'est par une interrogation sur les pouvoirs et les conditions du spectacle que passe aujourd'hui le chemin d'un théâtre de contestation.
>
> Bernard Dort, «L'Illusion politique,» *Politique hebdo*, 12 Jan. 1971, p. 18.

The Théâtre du Soleil confronts the problem of theater and revolution by questioning the conditions necessary for theater and by producing political plays. Inspired by the concept of revolution both as esthetic change and as government overthrow, the troupe challenges traditional notions about the theatrical institution.

The present group structure of the Théâtre du Soleil evolved over a period of six years. A change in the creative method and political orientation of the company took place simultaneously.

In 1964 the accomplished young director Ariane Mnouchkine brought together several of her former colleagues from the university company the «Association Théâtrale des Etudiants de Paris» (1). The group took the name «Théâtre du Soleil» in honor of the warm and luminous films of Jean Renoir and Max Ophüls and in reaction against the modish abbreviations of established theaters such as the Théâtre National Populaire (T.N.P.) or the Théâtre de l'Est Parisien (T.E.P.). Committing itself to the goals of the popular theater movement, the Théâtre du Soleil also opposed the existing theatrical institution by organizing as a workers' co-operative. Each of the members received the same salary and performed a variety of tasks (2).

That spring, the troupe of forty moved to a farm in the Ardèche where it began a strenuous work schedule of raising sheep, improvising, exercising, and rehearsing for its first production, Gorki's *Les Petits-Bourgeois.* Performed in Paris (1965), neither this play nor the second, an adaptation of Gauthier's *Le Capitaine Fracasse* (1966), brought the troupe to the public's attention. In 1966 the Théâtre du Soleil gave up its pastoral existence and moved back to Paris.

Commercial and critical success was won in 1967 with a production of Arnold Wesker's *The Kitchen.* Because it could find no other theater willing to house it, the company performed on the grounds of the Cirque de Montmartre. These performances drew raves from the public, as evidenced in Bertrand Poirot-Delpech's review: «Contentons-nous de retenir les réussites de Wesker et du Théâtre du Soleil parmi les plus importantes de la saison, les plus nouvelles, les plus inespérées» (3). The work on this play introduced the method the troupe would use to elaborate all its future productions: documentation and collective creation.

In order to understand the functioning of a kitchen staff, to capture its gestures and expressions, the actors went to the kitchens of several celebrated Parisian restaurants. They invited to their rehearsals chefs, butchers, dishwashers, and waiters, who advised and criticized them. Each actor worked on several roles at once. Parts were cast only at the end of several months of rehearsals. The entire company contributed to the final composition of each character and the play exuded a «collective rhythm and breathing» (4).

Mnouchkine and her company again animated the circus ground with their controversial winter 1968 adaptation of *A Midsummer Night's Dream*. One critic described the production as «*Le Songe* passé à travers Artaud» (5), for in its Dionysian interpretation of Shakespeare the Soleil attempted to open the doors of the public's subconscious. The luxurious fur-covered playing area and erotic acrobatics of the actors emphasized the troubling sexual undercurrents in the text, while dancers on leave from the Béjart Ballet Company infused the roles of Oberon and Titania with a perverse sensuality. Even the normally light-hearted aspects of the play were transformed into elements of pagan ritual with the woods fairies resembling Aztec chieftains and Puck, a twisted and diabolical spirit.

While searching for another location in which to continue *A Midsummer Night's Dream*, the Théâtre du Soleil experienced the beginning of the May '68 revolt. At the request of strike leaders, the troupe took a revival of *The Kitchen* to several of the occupied factories in the Parisian suburbs (6). The strikers' enthusiastic support of the workers portrayed in the play convinced the actors that theater really could contribute to the public's political consciousness.

After the May experience, the Théâtre du Soleil opted for a more critical theater in which the co-operative structure of the group would be affirmed. It acknowledged the limits of productions like *A Midsummer Night's Dream* in which both political efficacy and group creativity had been minimized:

Les événements de '68 nous ont apporté la confirmation de notre choix. La vie en groupe au sein de la Compagnie a suscité plus de responsabilités. *Le Songe d'une nuit d'été* a marqué une limite. C'était une erreur d'avoir accepté des comédiens de l'extérieur. . . . Depuis, nous avons instauré l'égalité des salaires, la connaissance collective. C'est un pas énorme dans la suppression de la notion même de hiérarchie (7).

The members decided that in the future they would marry the technique of collective creation with their increasingly leftist political orientation.

In speaking of the aftermath of May '68, Mnouchkine notes, «Plusieurs membres de la troupe et moi-même éprouvions une certaine lassitude sous l'influence de l'énorme atmosphère suicidaire qui a suivi l'après mai 1968» (8). To overcome its discouragement over the outcome of the May events, the Théâtre du Soleil in its next production examined one of the most difficult problems raised in May: the relationship of the artist to society. The actors adopted the clothing, gestures, and techniques of clowns in order to free their own personalities for analysis. Starting from «le degré zéro,» each actor improvised a series of autobiographical sketches in order to find a personal «clown,» or an incarnation of his own attitude as an artist toward society. Once these individual characters were created, two or three actors worked together to develop the basic skits which make up the work. Mnouchkine assumed the position of objective observer. Her criticism modified and refined the dialogue and action and perfected the final version of *Les Clowns* (1969). In creating *Les Clowns*, the members of the Théâtre du Soleil clarified their political position, for, despite the title of the work, the play repudiated the political impotence of artists.

By 1970, the Théâtre du Soleil had evolved into a fertile creative unit, radicalized to a large extent by the events of May and by its experience as a troupe on the fringe of the theatrical institution. It considered itself ready to concentrate on a collective creation with a political punch and logically enough chose to work on the theme of revolution. The resulting productions— *1789, La Révolution doit s'arrêter à la perfection du bonheur* (1970) and *1793, La Cité révolutionnaire est de ce monde* (1972)—attest to the maturity of the company's political and creative approach. As Mnouchkine states with regard to *1789*, «La forme du spectacle marque le départ d'une dramaturgie nouvelle, qui ne s'est pas imposée comme une révélation, mais représente l'aboutissement de notre formation commune» (9). An examination of these plays will point out how the Théâtre du Soleil deals with the question of theater and revolution by changing the creative process (and correspondingly the role of the actor) by interpreting the Revolution according to its own political viewpoint, and by experimenting with audience participation and political indoctrination.

To create *1789*, the actors first researched the subject matter and then initiated a nightly two-hour course on the Revolutionary period. Every evening following their performances of *The Kitchen*, a professor from the Sorbonne joined them to lecture and answer questions. They compiled an impressive documentation and bibliography, including Michelet's *Histoire de la Révolution française*, Albert Soboul's *Les Sans-culottes*, and Daniel Guérin's *La Lutte des classes sous la Première République*, from which they gleaned the themes and visual images for their first group of improvisations. This background also informed the original improvisations of *1793*.

The improvisations for both *1789* and *1793* extended over two six-month periods in which the actors invented their costumes, the characters, and the form of each play. For *1789*, the actors rehearsed in old costumes of their own or in cast-offs from other troupes, changing ribbons or hats to suit their improvisation and deriving personalized versions of their multiple roles. In *1793*, the actors created single characters based on an exploration of their own lives and family histories. Theater critic Colette Godard examined the result of this process and concluded, «Chaque comédien construit son personnage, et puisqu'il se choisit une existence en accord avec son caractère, il y est totalement impliqué» (10). The one actor-one character scheme of *1793* evolved during the course of the improvisations; the original plan had called for multiple roles as in *1789*. With the individualized characters came the need for a more concentrated scenic structure. The actors therefore devised a unified setting— a revolutionary assembly hall—for their performance.

The process of building a play on improvisations necessitated constant editing and criticism. Certain improvisations were eventually eliminated or changed. Rather than culminating in frustration for the actors involved, this method assured them that nothing they did was useless since each improvisation (including those rejected) was responsible for the genesis of another. This not only operated within one play, but carried over from one production to the next. A queuing-up sketch improvised for *1789* and later dropped was, for example, modified and eventually used in *1793*. Improvising allowed the actors to practice several acting styles, exploit their musical talents, and develop their directorial skills.

From *1789* to *1793* there was a marked increase in the individual actor's importance as editor and critic. Despite Mnouchkine's role as director and chief counselor, the actors assumed more and more responsibility for correcting their own improvisations and recognizing flaws in those of others. In creating *1793*, the actors had grown so aware of each others' capabilities that they could improvise in groups of twenty or more.

Faced with an endless expansion of formerly limited functions, the actor with the Théâtre du Soleil no longer conforms to age-old definitions of the dramatic artist, such as Louis Jouvet's conception of the actor as an antisocial monster who feigns adherence to another man's ideas. He resists social and artistic alienation not only by expressing his own political philosophy in the plays he performs but also by creating his own role. Louis Samier, a member of the troupe, explains, «je me sens comédien et je me trouve en accord avec ce que je fais et ce que je fais c'est moi . . . dans le spectacle et en dehors du spectacle» (11). The actor of the Soleil combines his social awareness and creative talents to equate the functions of actor and revolutionary.

In order to exercise their Marxist political predilection in *1789* and *1793*, the actors used a variety of techniques. Their first partisan act was the choice of the subject. Because they wanted to treat a topic familiar to all Frenchmen, they picked the French Revolution, «le seul patrimoine reçu par tous les Français» (12). However, as they disagreed with the textbook interpretation of the revolutionary events, they reinterpreted the conflict:

La Révolution, telle qu'on l'apprend dans les écoles primaires, est devenue une sorte de fable qui reste dans les mémoires sous formes d'images d'Epinal. Nous avons voulu la transcrire, à travers un spectacle, telle que nous la comprenions (13).

In *1789* and *1793,* the Théâtre du Soleil does not glorify the fearless revolutionaries but rather emphasizes the takeover of economic and political power by the bourgeoisie and the resulting oppression of the people. At the end of each performance, non-dramatized readings of statements which call for revolutionary action clearly propose a solution to the continuing domination of the bourgeoisie. Throughout the play, however, the troupe concentrates its political analysis on the characters.

In *1789* the actors play eighteenth-century fair comedians who, in turn, interpret the Revolution for the audience. The fair comedians mock the «villains»—Louis XVI, Marie-Antoinette, bourgeois representatives—through sarcastic introductions or burlesque portrayals, which include the use of various marionettes. Thus the King is represented by a hand puppet when he attempts to thwart the meeting of the Estates General; but when the Parisian women bring him to Paris from Versailles, he is shown as a larger-than-life marionette.

Within the overall spirit of derision, the fair comedians employ several different acting styles to present the characters of the Revolution. Several naturalistic—almost melodramatic—episodes evoke temporary moods of suspense, tragedy, or naive gaiety rather than resulting in mocking laughter. Throughout these diverse presentations, the Théâtre du Soleil indirectly comments on the lack of substance of the majority of the revolutionary characters by never portraying one figure more than once by the same actor. The unique exception is the revolutionary philosopher Jean-Paul Marat, who is uniformly presented and never ridiculed in costume or gesture. His revolutionary call agrees with the troupe's political stance.

The political position of the Théâtre du Soleil in *1793* does not, as in *1789*, emanate from outside the characters by denunciation and satire. It actually motivates the characters' actions. Each character is a member of a revolutionary people's organization involved in creating a new socialist community and is invested with the individual political opinion of the actor who created him. Therefore, the character Le Breton, designed by the actor Gérard Hardy (himself a political radical), is an *enragé* and follower of Jacques Roux, while the character Honoré Ferron, born of the more orthodox Marxist conscience of Jean-Claude Penchenet, is a legalist turned Babouvist. Criticism of the bourgeoisie takes the form of a political debate among the different revolutionaries.

In criticizing the wealthy classes at the time of the Revolution, the actors also condemn contemporary capitalist society, specifically alluding in each play to recent political problems. In *1793*, for example, the section members of the people's organization cite certain articles from the Declaration of the Rights of Man. Those quoted deal with moral questions under debate today. Article XIII condemns brutal or harsh treatment of criminal suspects: «Toute rigueur qui ne serait pas nécessaire pour s'assurer de sa personne doit être sévèrement réprimée par la loi» (p. 115). Its inclusion in the play alludes to the controversy over the methods of the French riot police and current prison practices in France. Both the tone and the style of *1789* and *1793* echo the evolving political mood of France. The popular festive ambiance of *1789* evokes the general vitality of the open street meetings of May 1968. The more meditative quality of the revolutionary committee meetings in *1793* bears witness to the sobering influence of May's aftermath.

This change not only corresponds to the contemporary political mood but also denotes the continuous political evolution of the actors, who found themselves increasingly politically committed from 1970 and the creation of *1789* to the 1972 opening of *1793*. In *1793* there is both a more positive approach to the revolution and a more clearly developed political ideology. While the subtitle of *1789*, St. Just's motto, «La révolution doit s'arrêter à la perfection du bonheur,» abstractly posits a future, intangible, even unattainable (because perfect) happiness, that of *1793*, «La cité révolutionnaire est de ce monde,» brings the problem back to the here and now. No longer dealing in a quasi-metaphysical speculation, the quotation indicates the troupe's belief that a change in government is possible in our time. Despite the defeat of the popular movement at the play's end, the concluding judgment, taken from Emmanuel Kant, supports the premise that an egalitarian society is inherent in the nature of man and that the struggle to achieve it cannot be contained:

Un tel phénomène dans l'histoire du monde ne s'oubliera jamais, car il a découvert au fond de la nature humaine une possibilité de progrès moral qu'aucun homme politique n'avait jusqu'à présent soupçonné. (p. 131)

1793 takes the leap of faith, no longer merely calling for civil war as does the character Gracchus Babeuf at the end of *1789* but declaring this war inevitable.

In *1793* the Théâtre du Soleil qualifies this revolutionary inevitability by demonstrating the necessity of political education. By the end of the play, the people conquer their ignorance and discover class struggle. This victory again indicates the evolving ideology of the troupe. In *1789* the villains are «l'aristocratie des nobles . . . remplacée par l'aristocratie des riches» (p.73). In *1793*, the danger comes from «l'aristocratie des représentants [qui succède] à l'aristocratie des nobles» (p. 125). By substituting the specific idea of «representatives» for *1789*'s more general term, «the rich,» *1793* not only postulates class struggle but also attacks the structure of representative government, opposing to it a direct democracy. In the play this is explained as a kind of utopian socialism in which the land would belong to all people: «Peut-être la terre pourrait être prise comme un grand bien communal de la nature où tous les êtres humains auraient un droit sur les productions qu'elle renferme» (p. 73).

Although the bourgeois representatives are also criticized in *1789*, the accusation is not leveled at the system of government but rather at the hegemony of the propertied classes. No character proposes a different political system. Moreover, the satire of the representatives constitutes only a portion of the general demystification of revolutionary mythology. In *1793*, on the contrary, the unique and central conflict occurs between the members of the popular assembly and a bourgeois representative to the Committee of Public Safety. After the latter's speech belittling the people's efforts, an army volunteer from Marseilles observes, «Il est beau *comme un roi!*» (p. 125). The analogy sums up the people's realization and the Théâtre du Soleil's conviction that a representative government can be as authoritarian as a monarchy.

To convince the public of the accuracy of its political position, the Théâtre du Soleil developed both a special set design and dramatic structure which experiment with the nature of audience participation. The sets of *1789* and *1793* follow the modern theatrical current of *la scène éclatée* or open theater, which the critic Gilles Sandier proclaims indispensable for a truly popular theater:

Depuis Mai, redisons-le, c'est pour quelques-uns, une évidence, et pour beaucoup, une idée acceptable, que nous ne pouvons plus donner à des expressions comme 'culture populaire' ou 'théâtre populaire' un autre sens que celui qui est lié à une révolution culturelle totale. Cette révolution, qui seule peut rendre un spectacle acceptable à ceux qui croient encore que le théâtre peut être un langage contemporain . . . a pour signe essentiel, au théâtre, la rupture avec l'ancien cadre clos de la représentation (14).

Open theater rejects the fourth-wall italianate stage which separates audience and actors. It utilizes environmental stage techniques to involve the spectator physically as well as emotionally in the play. The original material condition of the warehouse which serves as the locale of the Théâtre du Soleil was ideal for constructing an open theater, as the gutted factory had to be entirely rebuilt (15).

To construct the set for *1789*, the Soleil turned for inspiration to the tradition of medieval theater and popular fairs. It developed the following project: a rectangular stage consisting of five elevated platforms such as those used by carnival sideshows, with four wooden walkways connecting them. The decor includes a set of painted backdrops which can be attached to the rear of the platforms. These are changed according to the action of the play. The audience is composed of two groups, those who stand inside the platforms and those who sit outside on bleachers.

For the set of *1793*, the Théâtre du Soleil utilizes two different and separate structures. A platform-style stage, such as that in *1789*, serves as playing area for the first ten minutes of the performance. It provides a transition from the mood of *1789* to that of *1793*. On the platform, as in *1789*, the actors portray carnival barkers and fair comedians who sum up the events of 1789 for their audience. The remainder of the spectacle takes place in a different structure, the «Mauconseil Section Hall,» which the actors and audience enter by passing through a curtain from one nave of the theater to the other. This part of the

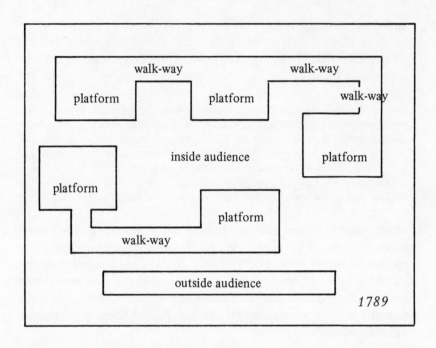

1789

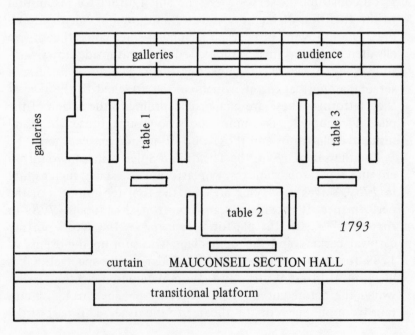

1793

MAUCONSEIL SECTION HALL

building is completely transformed into a huge assembly hall, with galleries lining two sides of the room. The galleries face three large table-and-bench groups, around and on which the players perform. The audience sits in the galleries or on the floor in front of the tables; it makes up a uniform body rather than two distinct audiences as in *1789.*

The sets of both *1789* and *1793* abolish the hierarchy of orchestra and balcony spectators, and, indeed, encompass the entire audience within the set design. The design, nevertheless, varies considerably from *1789* to *1793* because of the difference in the conception of the scenic space. In *1789* the scenic space is abstract. It represents an eighteenth-century open-air fair theater which is only invested with meaning when the actors perform. Furthermore, this meaning changes according to the stage action. The spectator must perceive the action in order to realize the play's dual dimension of theater-in-the-theater and 1789 revolutionary activity. In *1793,* on the contrary, the scenic space is a precise historical location, the Section Hall of the Mauconseil Assembly. It has a meaning before the action begins.

The utilization of the abstract space of one and the precise historical space of the other determines their respective complexity and simplicity. The carnivalesque set and staging of *1789* constantly surprises the public by its rapidly changing backdrops, blatantly varied lighting (from spots and pursuits to full house), and continuously differing floor patterns. The set and staging of *1793* reassures the spectator by remaining essentially the same. In *1793* the movement basically alternates from one table to another. The lighting, which imitates natural variations from dawn to dusk, contributes to the realistic aspect of the set. The audience is not, as in *1789,* constantly reminded of being in the theater.

Despite the concrete quality of the section hall in *1793,* its spatial unity is broken in several scenes. In two of these, for example, women section members wash their clothes at «the washhouse» (in the diagram—Table 3). Table 3 takes on the qualities of an imaginary wash-house outside the section hall. The public is therefore transported out of the physical boundaries which enclose it. These scenes disconcert the spectator, for, contrary to the transformable quality of the set of *1789*, the structural limitations of the set of *1793* prevent him from unquestioningly accepting spatial leaps.

The difference in the set design and staging of *1789* and *1793* calls for two different degrees of audience participation. In *1789*, the spectators who comprise the standing audience in the middle of the platforms fully participate in the action of the play. The actors address the spectators as if they were an eighteenth-century fair audience. The spectators therefore become actors in their own rights. Moving from one platform to another, following the action of the play, they are metamorphosed by the events of 1789 into the «people of Paris.» They celebrate the fall of the Bastille in a riotous kermesse. Urged on by the actors, they join hands, form a snake dance, take turns at games of chance and ring toss, and hobnob with a prancing bear. The frequent zigzagging of the actors throughout the audience engages the spectators' physical participation. They must step aside to allow the actors to pass or gather around them to hear the dialogue when the actors position themselves in their midst. In one scene, the public is forced to make way for a brusque procession of actors playing bourgeois representatives. Like the people of Paris with whom they identify, the audience succumbs to the inflated manners of the wealthy class. The spectators on the outside bleachers confirm the active role of the inside spectators by observing them just as they observe the professional actors.

In *1793* the audience is unified and, moreover, seated for the major part of the performance. It only physically participates in the play's action during the transitional ten-minute *parade*. As throughout *1789*, in the transitional phase of *1793* the spectators stand and the actors address them directly. When invited to join the actors for a revolutionary section meeting, the spectators rush into the section hall behind the transitional platform, momentarily «becoming» members of the section. However, this identification does not last as the audience is excluded from any further activity. The brief introductions at the beginning of each scene in *1793* are delivered in serious storyteller fashion by one of the section members, capturing the audience's attention but not provoking the rowdy and animated reactions which follow the carnival barkers' presentations in *1789*. Although the actors do occasionally walk through the audience, moving from one table to another, they never really disturb the spectators, nor do they interact with them, but rather contain the action among the performers.

The physical participation of the audience of *1789*, then, far surpasses that of the spectator of *1793*. In *1793* he is an observer, not an actor, while in *1789* he renounces his passivity, becoming creative in his own right. The excitement communicated through this participation in *1789* infects the seated audience, too. The spectator's physical participation also causes him to interact more with the rest of the audience.

The set design and text of both *1789* and *1793* were worked out simultaneously. Consequently the differences between the sets are reflected in the dramatic structure of the plays. As with the set design, a basic conception informs the dramatic structure of both plays—documentary theater.

Like the epic theater of Brecht, documentary theater, rather than building up to a climax, has a linear progression. Both *1789* and *1793* progress chronologically. Each scene is complete in itself. Documentary theater clarifies a social process instead of dramatizing a conflict between individuals or within one man. The characters are not defined by their individual psychology but considered according to their historical or political situation. Contrary to Buchner's romantic portrayal of the French Revolution in *La Mort de Danton*, which concentrates on the confrontation between the historical greats Robespierre and Danton, or Peter Weiss' *Marat/Sade*, which impartially opposes the revolutionary Marat to the *révolté* De Sade, *1789* and *1793* combine documentation with partisan imagination. Neither pessimistic (nothing can be done) nor overly optimistic (nothing need be tried), documentary theater transfers its political philosophy to the audience. It is up to the spectators to actualize the potential political explosion contained in the text.

The dramatic structures of *1789* and *1793* differ in their manner of communicating this need for political revolution. This difference corresponds to the elucidation of a different social process in each play. *1789* depicts the usurpation of power from the first and second estates by the bourgeoisie. The play concentrates on the evolution of opposing forces: from the people versus the nobility and the clergy to the people versus the bourgeoisie. In one of the first scenes of the play, an allegory presents the people revolting against the nobility, the clergy, and the King, while the closing allegory shows the people being defeated by the bourgeoisie. The triumph of the bourgeoisie becomes evident in its increasing presence on stage. The number of bourgeois characters dominates and finally eclipses those from the other social classes. With the developing power of the bourgeoisie, the tone of the play grows more solemn, the movement slower, and the colors less vivid. The vulgar appearance of a group of nineteenth-century bourgeois in the last scene of the play signals the consummation of their power and the crushing defeat of the people.

In *1793* the bourgeoisie serves as catalyst for the central concern of the play: the evolution of the political awareness of the people. The people, motivated by revolutionary sentiment at the beginning of the play, slowly realize through their contact with Baptiste Dumont, an arrogant bourgeois member of their revolutionary section, that their representatives, rather than standing for all the nation, form a new aristocracy. At the end of the play they therefore reject their original support of a representative system and demand direct democracy.

In both *1789* and *1793* the focus of the social process is the «people.» The presence of the people gives each play its unity. However, whereas the process elaborated in *1793* corresponds to the evolution of the people's political awareness, the process in *1789* escapes their understanding. If in *1793* the people's collective political consciousness dominates all the scenes and is the center of interest, in *1789* their homogeneity is found in their political «unconsciousness.» In *1789* the Soleil's point of view, which creates the overall tone of denunciation, might therefore be called the «people's point of view after the fact.» The people portrayed in the play have not yet acquired a definite political stance.

Indeed, the differing portraits of the people in *1789* preclude a unified political consciousness. Contrary to *1793*, in which the people, except for Baptiste Dumont, are the only characters, *1789* has a cast of characters belonging to several sociological groups, of which «the people» are but one. Unlike those in *1793*, the characters representing the people in *1789* are neither uniformly interpreted nor uniformly presented. Under the category «the people» can be grouped the peasants who appear intermittently throughout the play, the «Women of Paris» who appear only once, and a series of allegorical figures who appear in a variety of sketches, for example, «M. de Faubourg» whose aid is enlisted by a group of bourgeois merchants.

While the people in *1793* are optimistic and confident about their revolutionary duties, those of *1789* are often afraid and incapable of helping themselves. The peasants, who fall prey to the rumors about roving bandits spread by the aristocracy, react by fighting each other. The people in *1789* do not grasp the machinations of the other classes and continue to depend on their leadership. The celebrating Parisian women acquiesce to a bourgeois representative when he commands them to stop their festivities and return home. Section members in *1793* initiate a popular insurrection to protest bourgeois manipulation, but the women in *1789* refuse to revolt. Only Marat is in favor of a united popular front. He is, however, isolated both psychologically and physically from the people. Standing alone, he debates the bourgeois assembly in the play's closing contrapuntal exchange.

In *1793*, on the other hand, the section members appear together in all of the scenes, supporting the position of their comrades with cheers or shakes of the head. The one man who is excluded is the bourgeois representative. He appears in relatively few scenes and becomes less and less acceptable to the other section members as they become more politically aware. They finally exclude him from their group.

In only one instance—the central section of *1789*, which includes the taking of the Bastille and the victory celebration—do the people react strongly and *en masse* to their political situation. At this moment in the play, spectators from the standing audience and not professional actors represent the people. Incarnating Parisian revolutionaries, the spectators must «stop dancing and playing games and go home» when the character

Lafayette orders them to do so. The people-public are prompted to react angrily to this intrusion on their freedom.

The audience, therefore, directly experiences the ramifications of bourgeois oppression. Despite the obtuseness of the people throughout *1789*, the spectator cannot help but see the social process (the evolution from aristocratic to bourgeois power) develop. In *1789* the characters' lack of political awareness actually activates the spectators' consciousness. In *1793*, on the contrary, the social process centers on the characters' political awareness and depends on *their* activity. The elaboration of the process in *1793* allows the spectator to sit back and absorb the political message. That of *1789* actively engages him in the play. If, then, in one play the dramatic structure is controlled by the characters' political development, in the other, it is geared to develop the political consciousness of the spectators.

Political indoctrination takes place in many ways in *1789*. The Soleil quickly wins over the spectator to its point of view through the technique of denunciation. If the spectator does not accept the carnival barkers' attitude, he will, by inference, be siding with their target, thus relegating himself to a position of inferiority. Predisposed by theatrical convention to assent to the dominant mood, the spectator will usually not even question his immediate adherence, which will then be subconsciously strengthened by his identification with «those who know.» From the moment the fair comedians, in an early skit, mock the melodrama inherent in the royal family's flight to Varennes, the audience adopts a derisive approach as its own.

The Théâtre du Soleil's treatment of the different social classes in *1789* also arouses the spectators' enthusiasm for the people. Although the people are not particularly good, but rather helpless and harassed, the nobility, clergy, and bourgeoisie are definitely evil. The introductory series of allegories establishes this distinction in triplicate, as in all three the people bend under the pressure of the upper classes. The visual images strengthen the audience's adherence to the people's cause. The peasants resemble Le Nain portraits, the dark makeup circling their eyes bespeaking their poverty and hardship. The nobility and clergy, in outlandish costumes and ghoulish white makeup, with satanically-arched brows and red-stained lips, recall a host of bloodcurdling vampires. This stylization» prevents the audience's identification with almost all the characters. By contrast Marat, who is realistically portrayed, captures all the more the spectators' affection. His position as «hero» also reinforces the public's adherence to the people's cause.

1789 also increases the spectator's involvement in the play and his concern with the people's fate by appealing to his senses. The constantly and rapidly changing tableaux demand his attention at every moment, kaleidoscopically drawing him into the play's movement. The sustained barrage of sound engulfs him. The music, never meaningless, heightens the suspense, promotes the carnival atmosphere, or comments on the action. When the actors desire the greatest emotional response, they surround the standing audience with noise, as in the scene where peasant fathers strangle their babies rather than watch them starve. From all four of the platforms different groups of peasant couples scream in anger and pain at the spectators, stopping just before they become unbearable.

In addition to the sensory stimuli, a technique which may be called «intellectual reinforcement» also plays a substantial part in the Soleil's efforts to politicize the spectators. This method reaffirms fundamental political themes by repetition, by illustration, and by example. The statement «la Révolution est finie» appears three times in the play. Lafayette, head of the bourgeoisie's National Guard, says it first in order to terminate the celebration of the fall of the Bastille. Then a bourgeois member of the National Assembly proclaims it while invoking martial law. Finally Barnave, formerly the Queen's confidant, declares the end of the Revolution in order to calm his new masters, the bourgeoisie. The phrase always marks the end of a different popular victory and emphasizes, through the changing spokesmen, the increasing domination of the middle class.

The hierarchical nature of bourgeois power is conceptualized in the vignette «les Cahiers de doléances.» The King proclaims that all Frenchmen shall have the opportunity to communicate their needs to him. In a theatrical *tour de force*, two actors portray consecutively a tenant farmer, an important cultivator, a

pharmacist, and a parliamentary representative who have prepared petitions to the King. Each succeeding portrait is characterized by a more refined accent, a more voluminous stomach, a
more elegant mode of transportation, and a more avaricious nature. Each man entrusts his petition to his «better,» but only the
representative's finally arrives at Court.

By treating the most important political themes in more than
one manner, the Théâtre du Soleil lends salience to its criticism
of bourgeois power. The troupe twice illustrates the discrepancy
between the bourgeoisie's conception of equal rights and its notion of property rights. In a realistically staged assembly debate
on the rights of man a representative cunningly delineates «natural» rights. His statement, which illogically proves that inequality is natural, is a direct transcription of a debate which occurred
on the Assembly floor in 1789:

Pour assurer sa conservation et se procurer le bien-être chaque homme tient
de la nature des facultés. C'est dans le plein et entier exercice de ces facultés que consiste la liberté.

De l'usage de ces facultés dérive le droit de propriété.

Chaque homme a un droit égal à sa liberté et à sa propriété.

Mais chaque homme n'a pas reçu de la nature les mêmes moyens pour user
de ses droits, de là naît l'inégalité entre les hommes. *L'inégalité est donc
dans la nature même.* (p.64)

Men are «naturally unequal.» Some men can be considered equal
only to property.

The satirical vignette which follows the debate illustrates the
thesis that people are equal to property. A paste-complexioned,
white-garbed planter and his mulatto neighbor Mlle Adélaïde,
indolently rock back and forth on their verandas in Santo Do-
mingo. Their female slaves fan them or scratch their heads on
command. Suddenly, a Parisian envoy arrives to convey the Declaration of the Rights of Man. The negresses' exultation at hear-
ing themselves called naturally free and equal is squelched when
the planter informs them, «on a parlé des hommes, mes dou-
dous, pas des nègres» (p.66). So as not to confuse racial preju-

dice with property rights, Mlle Adélaïde and the planter, the two *land owners*, go off to take tea together in order to celebrate their «new found» equality.

1789 fuses intellectual reinforcement with emotional and physical participation in order to involve the spectator totally in the play, thus convincing him of its political viewpoint. The constant changes in movement, style and mood work on both conscious and unconscious levels to win his support. The spectator is caught up in the play's wealth, its multiplicity of signs, expanding images, and exuberance.

1793, on the contrary, attempts to politicize the audience by appealing particularly to its critical sense. The spectator's modest degree of physical participation corresponds to a measured exposition of the play's philosophy. The characters bear almost the entire responsibility for transferring to the audience the political message. Realistically portrayed, they have neither the flexibility nor the sign value of the characters in *1789*. Their costumes, although they indicate their social position, do not symbolize their psychology or the actors' opinion of them. The socialist message is communicated uniquely through dialogue and narrative.

Narrative or *récit* alternates with dialogue in each of the ten major vignettes of *1793*. The narrative style predominates, taking three distinct forms throughout the play. One is the short introductory *récit*, which situates each vignette in time and place. The second, similar to the introductory *récit*, is a simple narrative which offers either an historical commentary or documentary information. This simple narrative often closes the vignettes. The third and most important is the dramatized *récit*. The actors of the Théâtre du Soleil indicate their political position by enthusiastically dramatizing all the popular victories while simply narrating the people's defeats, such as the Terror and the end of the *sans-culottes* movement. Pantomimes, gymnastics, and symbolic sketches bring to life the narrative, as in the Valmy episode. While relating the events of the battle to the section members, the heroes of Valmy impersonate Prussian and French soldiers and act out the conflict. In the dramatized *récits*, the section members perform for each other rather than for the audience.

The constant presence of all the actors on stage reacting to the various recitations sets up a continuous dialogue. This is particularly apparent in the case of the women, who form a domestic chorus. They comment on the political activities of the men in short sketches which illustrate the daily problems of hunger and shelter and make palpable the privations of the section members.

In contrast to the sensory pummeling in *1789*, in *1793* musical emotionalism is confined to a melodramatic Berlioz piece which coincides with the transitional parade. With one other exception, a drum-roll which paces a sketch on firearms training, the play excludes musical reinforcement. Once in the section hall, the section members themselves play instruments or sing only when called on by their comrades. Music is therefore integrated into their activities, such as the recital which celebrates the Valmy victory.

Lighting replaces music as a source of political commentary. For the dramatized *récit* of the capture of the Tuileries, bright sunlight illuminates the section hall corresponding to the section members' happiness and the approval of the Théâtre du Soleil. During the narration of the deaths of several of the section members as a result of the Convention's triumph, the lights grow dimmer and dimmer, signaling the collapse of the popular movement. Near total darkness envelops the *récit* of the Terror.

When, in *1793*, the Théâtre du Soleil wishes to illustrate the central conflict, it completely renounces the subtlety of lighting effects to construct class struggle before the spectators' eyes. In two of the last scenes of the play, Baptiste Dumont and the section members stand facing each other on separate tables. The bourgeois representative is thus both spatially and ideologically distanced.

1793, rather than being oriented toward immediate pleasure and political adherence as is *1789*, is geared toward reflection and meditation. The spectator, separated from the production by a lack of physical participation, excluded from the section members' intimacy, and relatively undisturbed by sensory stimuli, can concentrate solely on the ideas which the section members present.

Open theater and documentary theater do not, therefore, necessarily coincide with direct audience participation. The degree of spectator involvement depends on how these forms are exploited. *1789* attempts to engage the spectator on as many levels as possible. *1793* attempts to disengage him. Bertrand Poirot-Delpech summarizes the difference between the two:

1793 ne fait que montrer de la parole en action et comment une poignée de sectionnaires produisent de la pensée révolutionnaire de l'utopie.

Avec *1789* la Révolution a quitté la grisaille sournoise de manuels pour se refaire image en mouvement, espoir en marche, élan de masse, joie de foule, jeu forain, cortège, farandole (16).

Each approach is meant to convince the spectators of the wisdom of the Théâtre du Soleil's anti-Establishment philosophy.

Of the two plays, *1793* is the least cogent as it sometimes borders on the polemic. This reflects the growing commitment of the troupe, which has become more politicized through the performance of political plays (17). Proselytizing, however, must be controlled in order to respect theatrical limits. *1793* partially fails as a political weapon precisely because of its flaws as a dramatic piece.

In *1793* the actors are so absorbed that they lose the power of denunciation which gives life to *1789*. By making no attempt to involve the spectators in *1793*, the actors risk alienating the audience, particularly those spectators whose political apathy precludes their sympathy. Despite the number of dramatized *récits* the play drags, hampered by a limited movement and a lack of mythical imagery. Furthermore, the confrontation between the section members and Baptiste Dumont does not adequately illustrate the people-bourgeois conflict. As a fictional creation, Baptiste Dumont is weak and lifeless. He is made to speak a barrage of documentary material which is not only didactic but also ambiguous, and he is therefore an unconvincing foil for the people's projects. That his role was written, rather than created through improvisations, largely explains its drabness but does not excuse its ineptitude.

No such weaknesses lessen the political thrust of *1789*. The visual images, music, lighting, juxtaposition of acting styles, and dialogue spring from a unique concern to make the audience aware of the dichotomy between the potential of the Revolution and its actualization. In contrast with *1793*, it is a theater of signs, one which the actor Michel Lonsdale calls «le seul théâtre qui compte aujourd'hui» (18). Excellently suited to contemporary audiences, the techniques on which *1789* is built nevertheless span theatrical history. In it, the Théâtre du Soleil spares almost no dramatic tricks. Moving from guignol to parody to bacchic dance and heated debate, the actors delve into nearly all of the theater's possibilities, crowning this experience by presenting theater-on-theater. The greater success of *1789* leads therefore to the conclusion that, by being the most «theatrical,» theater can also be the most politically effective.

In its latest collective creation, *L'Age d'or* (1975-1976), the Théâtre du Soleil explores the extreme theatricality of commedia dell'arte and Chinese theater to create a satirical piece on contemporary society. Eight sequences illustrate what the troupe considers to be the most crucial problems of the reality of the 1970's or «l'age de l'or» (the reign of gold): building scandals, unwanted children, drug abuse, non-communication, economic exploitation. A closing fantasy portrays the apocalyptic end of the Establishment, thereby paving the way for «l'age d'or» (the golden age) or a totally egalitarian society. The story of the arrival, life, and death in France of an Arab worker loosely holds together the disparate elements of the play.

Much as *Les Clowns*, *L'Age d'or* owes its dramatic strength to the inventiveness of individual actors. After conducting a series of discussions about their problems and hopes with scores of high school students, housewives, and workers, the actors sought equivalents for twentieth-century types (the immigrant, the feminist, the big businessman) among the stylized characters of the commedia and Chinese theater. In the Soleil's production Harlequin became «Abdallah,» the naive immigrant worker and eternal scapegoat. Pantaloon is transformed into «Marcel Pantalon,» a real estate wheeler dealer and eternal villain. Improvising led to the creation of episodes in which the interactions of these contemporary *lazzi* expose the social injustices of the capitalist system.

The set design continues the open theater experimentation begun with *1789*. The performance space is again an abstract one, consisting of a series of burlap-covered hills and valleys which the audience must climb up and slide down as it follows the play's action. A copper-covered ceiling, fitted with thousands of tiny white lights, bathes the playing area in warmth, helping to establish a good-humored camaraderie between spectators and actors.

In performance, the actors define through mime and acrobatics their emotions and their environment. They provide introductions and musical accompaniment, and sometimes hold spotlights on each other. Constantly improvising, they modify the show from one performance to the next. To indicate this «theater in progress» aspect of the play, the Soleil has subtitled *L'Age d'or* a «first draft.»

Paradoxically, this «theater in progress» aspect—responsible for the excitement of the performance—is also its principal failure. The lack of structural unity and balance detracts from the philosophical coherence of the play. At times, the spectator has the impression of floating between witty but unconnected images. He is rarely emotionally involved in the action. The unfinished quality therefore diminishes the political impact of the performance. Now that it has pushed theatricality to the extreme, it is perhaps time for the Soleil to find a style which marries theatricality to a precise political theme.

Chapter V

ANDRE BENEDETTO: RITUAL AND REVOLUTION

Je suis né dans la dent de sagesse du Christ
Dans la machoire de Karl Marx
André Benedetto, «Autocritique,» *Urgent Crieur* (Paris: P.J. Oswald, 1966),
p. 73.

May '68 provided a focus which raised the political consciousness of an entire generation of artists. André Benedetto, however,
anticipated the movement by a full two years. He first proclaimed a personal declaration of independence from estheticism
in his 1966 collection of poems, *Urgent Crieur*, in which he condemns those poets who are merely «polisseurs de cailloux»
(p. 66). Carrying out the fundamental principle of his personal
art poétique: «Apprendre le mot Colère et prendre le vers aux
dents» (p. 64), he denounces social ills and artistic hypocrisies
in a series of brusque poems, remarkable for their hammered
rhythm and brutal images. Like Rimbaud he cries out against a
sordid existence, but he counters the former's revolutionary appraisal: «La vraie vie est ailleurs,» with «La vraie vie est ici. / Ici

entre les quatre murs» (p. 44). Rather than advocate escape, Benedetto challenges the poet to come to grips with the disquieting reality of the here and now.

Seven months later, in the April manifesto (1) of his theater troupe, the Nouvelle Compagnie d'Avignon, he challenges the «here and now» of French theater:

Le théâtre aujourd'hui s'appelle 007, gaz délétère, hilarant et paralysant, et asphyxiant. Il est là pour tuer lentement, pour tuer à petit feu, pour entretenir l'espoir quand il n'y a plus d'espoir d'aucune sorte. Heureux ceux qui attendent Godot et ils sont nombreux, trop nombreux encore.

Dismissing consecutively metaphysical theater, experimental theater, and popular theater (as inscribed in the Vilaresque tradition of public service), Benedetto proposes a revolutionary theater which will cease trying to unite its public but rather help «blow the top» off social conventions: «Nous avons à nous battre contre toutes les formes d'oppression. Ne serait-ce que pour respirer un peu mieux.» He aims his attack not only at the reigning social and economic structure, capitalism, but also at the deadening effect of this system on the human spirit: «Il y a trop de chaînes, et sur nous et en nous qui nous scellent les circonvolutions cérébrales.»

Once again he dedicates the poet to the task:

C'est un combat qui exige un rare sérieux et une conscience assez haute de la fonction du poète. On veut nous faire croire qu'il a pu être jadis un conciliateur. De toute façon aujourd'hui, il sera l'anti-conciliateur, c'est-à-dire tout autre chose qu'un montreur de galaxies.

Casting the dramatic poet as a revolutionary *meneur de jeu*, Benedetto exhorts him not to lead the way to some celestial paradise but rather to inspire the fight against terrestrial oppression. Both in his meta-theatrical activities and in his dramatic creations, Benedetto personally fulfills this role.

After the publication of his 1966 theater manifesto, Benedetto renounced his status quo position as pillar of decentralization. Refusing to continue supplying cultural provender to the Avignon public, he transformed his two hundred-seat Théâtre des Carmes into a center of politicized theatrical activity. He rejected the cultural guidebook format of the company's three-year-old review, *Soirées*, and chose instead to publish Marxist doctrine and accounts of the company's activities.

Numerous young Avignonnais, including Gérard Gélas, who later formed his own politically committed troupe, Le Chêne Noir, joined him in weekend sessions designed to examine the political role of art. Benedetto animated happenings involving the local population (*Sonorités*, 1967), parades commemorating the Commune (1971) and opposing the Vietnam War (1972), and street theater in support of striking railroad workers (*Les Cheminots en grève*, 1971). In 1971, he also invited the townspeople to collaborate on a play about Avignon. This resulted in a lively satirical review focused on the Papal Palace, *A bec et à griffes.*

His company performed not only in Avignon, but also on tour throughout the south of France, in Italy, Switzerland, and Poland. This prolific activity helped establish ties with several foreign troupes interested in political theater. Benedetto's plays have consequently been translated into Japanese, English, Arabic, Spanish, and Italian (2).

Largely through Benedetto's initiative, an unofficial «off» theater sprang up in the summer of 1966 beside the official Avignon drama festival. To protest against the concept of «official culture,» the Nouvelle Compagnie and other marginal troupes gathered in Avignon during the festival month to produce their own, often controversial, works. Today little differentiation is made between «in» and «off» festivals, except for the majestic setting of the official performing areas, the Palais des Papes and the Cloître des Carmes. The «off» theater has surpassed the official productions in inventiveness and critical interest, while the «in» plays have adopted political themes as their own.

When Benedetto agreed in 1973 to enter the official festival by way of the Cloître des Carmes, he did so without fearing to upset the balance between «in» and «off.» More important, his participation allowed him to be able to sponsor, two doors away in his unoccupied theater, an unofficial Occitanian national liberation festival (3). An Occitanian himself (Benedetto was born in Salon, near Avignon, in 1935), he has been interested in the

Occitanian movement since its radicalization in 1968. The movement's demand for recognition and renewal of Provençal literature and language as well as for economic independence prompted Benedetto to invite Occitanians to Avignon in order to discuss the propagation of their culture throughout France and the liberation of their economy from northern interests. Under his direction, the Occitanian festival committee published a daily newspaper, *Esclarmonda* (esclar = to enlighten; monda = the people), with articles in both Occitanian and French. He also promoted a series of programs featuring Provençal singers and dancers. Two theatrical troupes, the Centre Dramatique Occitan de Provence and the Théâtre de la Carriera, performed agit-prop sketches in Occitanian on the «colonization» of the South. Benedetto himself maintained the spirit of the counter-festival in his own plays, *La Madone des Ordures: Nostra Dona dei Bordilhas* and *Comment et pourquoi on fait un assassin de Gaston D.* (4). His 1974 production, *Géronimo*, continued to censure the colonization of Occitania by equating the Occitanian peasant with the Apache warrior. All three works contain long passages in Occitanian and treat specific Occitanian problems.

His interest in the Occitanian movement led Benedetto to animate a regional festival in 1974. Working from March until May in collaboration with the people of Montauban, he created *Le Siège de Montauban*, an historical fresco dating from the city's heroic resistance to the armies of Louis XIII to contemporary times. In July, townsmen performed the play in the market place of Montauban. Benedetto terms the experience an «urban psychodrama.»

Occitania is the latest of four major subject areas on which Benedetto concentrates in his more than twenty post-manifesto productions. The others include the Vietnam War, political revolution, and class struggle under capitalism. In addition to the four major works on Occitania, he has produced *Napalm* (1967), *La Chine entre à l'O.N.U.* (1971), and *Chant Funèbre pour un soldat américain* (1972) which deal with Vietnam; *Le Petit Train de M. Kamodé* (1969), *Emballage* (1970), *Histoire d'un œuf* (1972), and *Les Tambours de Satan* (1973) which treat class struggle; and *Zone Rouge* (1968), *Rosa Lux* (1970), *La*

Commune de Paris (1971) and *Alexandra K* (1975) which embody revolutionary fervor.

He has deliberately eliminated from his repertoire the classical and modern works which dominated it from 1961 to 1966 (5) in order to examine those themes which inform the contemporary consciousness. Writing in osmosis with current events, he gives his own political interpretation of them. For example, two months after China's admission to the United Nations, he created *La Chine entre à l'O.N.U.*, a sarcastic portrayal of American foreign policy in Vietnam, in which Vietcong pressure on the American government forces Nixon and Kissinger to accept China's entry. His present interest in Occitania parallels the emergence on the national scene of the liberation movement. Despite his Occitanian roots he only learned to speak and write Occitanian in 1971.

More interesting than Benedetto's subject matter is his dramatic form, for the creation of a unique theatrical structure is his prime means of combatting spiritual and political constraints: «C'est au niveau de la forme, dans ce qui constitue la matière du spectacle, langage, jeu des acteurs, dramaturgie, qu'il faut rompre avec l'idéologie dominante» (6). Form takes precedence over content in Benedetto's dramatic practice. As he notes, «Le danger [du théâtre révolutionnaire] serait en effet de continuer à pratiquer le théâtre de la vieille société sans rien commencer à modifier dans le théâtre lui-même» (7). An examination of three of Benedetto's most characteristic and most successful plays, *Napalm, Le Petit Train de M. Kamodé,* and *La Madone des Ordures*, will reveal the Benedettian dramatic form and establish the relationship of this form to the political impact of his theater.

Napalm, one of his first post-manifesto plays and the first French play on Vietnam, is a multi-faceted free verse creation in which Benedetto fiercely denounces American involvement in Vietnam (8). Its thirty-three vignettes vary from poetic sorcerers' rounds and verbal sparring matches to pantomime, a lyrical love ballad, and even a superficially nonsensical song and dance routine by Mic-*Key* Mouse:

Je suis le mec le mac le mic
Key à Minnie
Et le pote à Dingo
J'ai pris le pouvoir à Saigon
Tout le monde s'est aperçu
Et ça n'a rien changé (p. 43)

This panoply of scenic styles can be divided into two main types, satirical and ritualistic. The satire is principally directed at the broadly caricatured American dignitaries, President Johnson and Defense Secretary MacNamara. Both their attitudes and their proclamations parody the early policy stand of the United States in Vietnam and the tactics of the American government there. A boastful Johnson, for example, cannot understand why he has not yet won the war. After all, «Le Vietnam n'est pas un pays, c'est un problème. Sans la guerre il n'y aurait pas de Vietnam!» (p. 115). And MacNamara, totally perplexed, complains that even with his «dizaines d'ordinateurs électroniques» (p. 107) he cannot count all the Vietcong.

The most damning accusation against American aggression occurs in the ritualistic vignettes which constitute the major portion of the play. In addition to several ritualistic scenes scattered among the satirical sketches, ritual dominates the central section of extreme violence and physicality in which the shocking visual images and poetic frenzy contrast sharply with the intellectualized satirical portraits of Johnson and MacNamara. Framed by the story of a captured American pilot, the ritual sequence depicts the most gruesome and irrational aspects of America's participation in the war. When, for example, the pilot stands up in scene sixteen to address his Vietnamese captors, he is no longer himself but a reincarnation of Charles Whitman, the Texas sniper who killed eighteen people from an Austin tower in 1966. In a long entranced monologue, he works himself into a homocidal fury, clearly establishing a parallel between Whitman's sickness and the psychology behind America's efforts in Vietnam:

Bientôt midi je vais tirer
Comme le soleil des rayons,
Au beau milieu de la journée
Au soleil de midi tirer

Sur tout ce qui bouge à Austin
Sur tout ce qui bouge à Dallas
Sur tout ce qui bouge à Danang (p.60)

A series of human metamorphoses linking one scene to the next maintains the ritual form throughout the sequence. When Whitman concludes his monologue and turns to shoot at his listeners, he again becomes an air force bomber, dropping napalm on a Vietnamese village. The Vietcong soldiers who have captured him become, in turn, villagers who run for shelter from the attack. One of them, the small child Vinh, is struck before she reaches safety. This produces a paroxistic reaction in which, contorted and screaming, she chants:

J'ai les pieds brûlés
J'ai les jambes brûlées
J'ai les cuisses brûlées
. . . .
J'ai la cervelle qui brûle
Tout brûle Tout brûle Tout brûle (p.67)

The others join her, shouting again and again the word «napalm» at the audience.

The next transformation finds the wounded child's father changed into an American Quaker about to immolate himself with the aid of his daughter (formerly Vinh). Before he completes his sacrifice to cleanse American guilt—«Je suis le fanal de la justice!» (p. 70)—he is metamorphosed into a Buddhist, burning his body not only to protest against the war but also to free his soul for physical combat: «Que je renaisse pour me battre . . . Contre ceux qui me font brûler» (p. 77).

The horror inherent in these two complementary scenes is multiplied many times over in the ribaldry of the American soldiers who then emerge in the place of the sacrificial participants. The immolation becomes part of a theatrical game the soldiers play in which they mock the Vietnamese. The G.I.'s end their parody with a bloody torture scene. The ritual movement terminates when the soldiers, in turn, are transformed into Vietcong guerillas miming the capture of the pilot.

Benedetto both encloses and permeates his condemnation of

American aggression with a reflection on the relationship between literature and politics. The play begins with the now historic epistolary exchange between Soviet poet Yevgeny Yevtushenko and American novelist John Steinbeck. Yevtushenko addresses his «cher vieux John,» praising him for his past activism and demanding why now at a time when American pilots bomb Vietnamese children, he says nothing: «Est-il possible que vos 'Raisins de la Colère' / Soient désséchés?» (p. 11). Steinbeck urbanely replies that even though politics are dirty, he will be glad to denounce American involvement in the war if Yevtushenko will criticize China's and Russia's role.

In the succeeding scenes, Benedetto condemns Steinbeck's non-partisan attitude and his naive confidence in America by utilizing a theater-in-theater structure which allows the «Vietnamese» to speak for themselves. Although the play begins with Benedetto's company performing their interpretation of the Vietnam war, they soon transform themselves into the Vietnamese «Ensemble Artistique de l'Armée de Libération.» Otherwise, they worry, «Nous risquons de passer devant la Commission des Activités Anti-américaines. Nous pourrions recevoir une bombe sur le théâtre sous prétexte qu'il est situé au Nord-Vietnam» (p. 32). Painting yellow circles on their faces and slanted lines at the corners of their eyes, the French actors become «Vietnamese actors» playing the roles of Johnson, MacNamara, the pilot, Vietcong and American soldiers, and the various secondary or choral figures. They also begin interacting with the audience as if it too were Vietnamese attending a performance of a Vietcong dramatic troupe.

The theater-in-theater structure develops yet another dimension in the last three scenes of the play. MacNamara briefs Johnson that American writers have begun protesting against the war. Johnson laments:

> Où sont nos Hemingway, nos Walt Whitman?
> Qui portaient leur sexe en sautoir
> Leurs colombes en bandoulière. (p. 133)

Although disappointed, the President finds nothing frightening in the C.I.A. discovery of anti-war literature. Indeed, he decides to read aloud a protest drama, playing himself in the role of «Johnson,» while MacNamara plays that of «MacNamara.» In the last scene of the newly unearthed script, «Johnson» and «MacNamara» order the atomic annihilation of Washington, D.C.

The President and his Defense Secretary then step aside, out of their roles, to watch this destruction materialize before their eyes. The other actors, in a final ritual, portray the apocalyptic end of the Capital. They twitch spasmodically, fall on the stage, moan, scream, and finally expire. At the last gasp of the last victim, Johnson turns to MacNamara and exults, «Le théâtre . . . c'est quand même un fameux passe-temps» (p. 148).

The juxtaposition of the positive horror of the apocalypse and Johnson's insensitivity to it epitomizes Benedetto's criticism of the United States. It also communicates to the audience the author's position on the effectiveness of political theater, for despite Johnson's emotional vacuity, the spectators cannot help but be disturbed by the savage ending. Comparing Johnson's reaction with their own, they are further alienated from him. His appreciation of the theater as merely a pleasant pastime appears both morally repugnant and contrary to their own experience.

The spectators are affected throughout the play by the anguish communicated in the ritualistic scenes. In them, Benedetto seems to exorcise his own anger against the war while transferring it to the audience through the intermediary of the «Vietnamese players.» Having established a bond of direct address, Benedetto invites the public to participate in his theatrical rite. However, he cancels a possible catharsis by breaking up the ritual with satire, multiplying the theater-in-theater techniques, and generally never allowing the audience to forget that it is attending a theatrical performance. At the play's end, the audience must deal intellectually with the emotional havoc wrought by the ritual. They are to take up the work of exorcism in real life.

As with *Napalm*, in *Le Petit Train de M. Kamodé* Benedetto uses free-verse ritual to denounce his political enemies. And once again he explores the consequences of political theater. However, contrary to *Napalm*, in *Le Petit Train de M. Kamodé* Benedetto infuses ritual with satire, rather than separating the two. Furthermore, *Le Petit Train de M. Kamodé* has an additional didactic dimension which differentiates it from *Napalm* (9). Whereas *Napalm* uses ritual to criticize, *Le Petit Train de M. Kamodé* uses it to educate. The superstructure of the play can therefore be interpreted as a rite of passage into a Marxist universe.

To illustrate the injustice of state monopoly capitalism (le *K*apitolism *M*onopolist *d'É*tat or KAMODE), Benedetto chooses the French national railroad system. As in *Napalm*, he depends on symbolic props, representative figures, songs, dances, and poetry to communicate his message. The play takes place on a white hexagon representing a map of France, while the opposing interests are allegorized as M. Kamodé, a villainous blue dwarf in a business suit, and as Peuple, a heroic red giant in welder's overalls. The essentially melodramatic plot concerns Peuple's efforts to wrest Arachné, the poetic personification of the Société Nationale des Chemins de Fer Français (S.N.C.F.) from Kamodé's grasp.

The play begins with a burlesque military rite in which Kamodé and his «Etat-Major»: Signal d'Alarme (the public opinion counselor), Règle à Calcul (the profit consultant), and Ecran de Fumée (the propaganda wizard) are introduced to the audience. Kamodé happily dances and sings of his undisputed power while manipulating a chorus of wooden puppets, his collaborators (kamodéllaborateurs):

> Et tout ça usine
> Et tout ça échine
> Et tout ça turbine
> pour moi! (p. 26)

The «Etat-Major» intones the exploiter's creed and dutifully kowtows to their chief.

From the midst of this self-congratulatory orgy, Peuple emerges «sain de corps et d'esprit.» Although Ecran de Fumée momentarily succeeds in hypnotizing him with a patriotic tirade,

Peuple reawakens and begins his campaign to exorcise Kamodé's domination over the working masses. He rallies the workers
by singing the «song of the oppressed,» followed by a love duo
with Arachné:

> Toi pillée, moi pillé
> Arachné, mon amour
> C'est nous le couple de demain. (p. 38)

This first predominantly satirical part ends in a «march of progress.» Kamodé and cohorts, having repulsed Peuple's onslaught
for the third time, parade across the stage in jubilant homage to
profit, capitalism, and each other.

The second, more didactic part is dominated by an exposé of
the Kamodé system and Peuple's revolutionary cry:

> Nous voulons mettre fin
> A la propriété privée des moyens de production
> Nous voulons que la voie ferrée ne soit pas
> Au service exclusif des monopoles
> Mais au service du public. (p. 89)

Long lyrical passages, in which Peuple eulogizes the railway in
the person of Arachné, balance and complement the extensive
didacticism. Peuple glorifies her as «le cheval espoir,» «l'étalon
capable de voler jusqu'au ciel» (p. 82). In his romantic appraisal
of Arachné, Peuple rejects the law of supply and demand. He
even finds her most attractive when least profitable.

Peuple's poetic lack of business acumen naturally does not
charm M. Kamodé: «Tout ça c'est de la poésie / De la rigolade
on s'en fout» (p. 86). Only interested in cash-in-hand profits, he
rejects Peuple's belief in the «homme nouveau» and the «vaste
paradis sur terre» (p. 105) promised by a socialist system. Kamodé cannot, however, compete with the snowballing effect of
Peuple's enthusiasm: «Vous allez me massacrer / Me mettre en
bouillie / Avec vos arguments!» (p. 87). Peuple even wins over
to his side Règle à Calcul and Signal d'Alarme. At the play's end,
an isolated Kamodé is forced to vanish in the cloud of his own
rhetoric. Peuple thus completes the exorcism begun in the first
part of the play.

To reinforce the lesson behind Kamodé's disappearance, Benedetto includes a symbolic spectator, M. Dupont, among the characters. M. Dupont, «le bon français moyen,» holds the central position in the play, for almost all the action is directed at him. As the observer who follows the Peuple-Kamodé struggle, he is subjected to Kamodé's cajoling and Peuple's scolding. At the beginning of the play he submissively accepts Kamodé's system:

> Je suis un bon bougre
> Je fais ce qu'il faut
> Je participe je ne dis pas grand'chose (p. 33)

However, under the guidance of Peuple, whose lyrical flights attract him far more than Kamodé's doggerel, Dupont undergoes the Marxist initiation rite. He gradually understands that Kamodé's claim to power is mere fiction; and by the play's end he becomes an anti-capitalist activist:

> Je viens en spectateur
> Je me retrouve acteur
> Et maintenant je distribue des tracts
> Et je fais de la politique (p. 112)

This, concludes Peuple with satisfaction, is the role of theater in class struggle.

A symbolic substitute for the real spectators, Dupont serves as intermediary for their own political consciousness-raising. After Dupont has finally joined «la cause du Peuple,» Benedetto focuses the initiation rite on the audience itself. No longer preoccupied with the ritual spectator, Benedetto has Peuple address the public directly, encouraging it to join Arachné on stage in a solidarity dance.

Entrance and exit corridors, by which the audience passes to and from the playing area, perfectly duplicate Dupont's experience. The entrance or «couloir de la mort lente» is antiseptic and cold, with business-like hostesses demanding complete cooperation from the spectators. This is Kamodé's domain. The exit, or «couloir de la vie retrouvée,» is colorful and non-structured. Friendly guides organize games and invite the spectators to discuss Kamodé's future. This is the domain of the liberated Marxist. This is also the corridor which leads out to the street.

With the street proposed as the final destination, Benedetto once again shifts the responsibility of action from the play to the spectators. As in *Napalm*, the ritualistic aspect of the work has its own limitations. Even Dupont, who has been transformed by the ritual, realizes that being initiated is only the beginning of political liberation. The struggle commences when class consciousness is achieved.

La Madone des Ordures is both a spoken and sung Occitanian *chanson de geste* and a ritual invoking the birth of the Occitanian revolutionary. Like *Napalm* and *Le Petit Train de M. Kamodé*, the play combines satire and didacticism with poetic ritual. As a *chanson de geste*, the action traces the emigration of an Occitanian peasant family across the impoverished southern tip of France. A mother and her two sons, Joan and Peire, are forced to sell their farm in order to pay off their debts. Loading their few possessions into a rickety 2 CV Citroën (*deux-chevaux*), they leave Nîmes to start a new life elsewhere in Provence. Successive sojourns in Saint-Gilles, Saintes-Maries-de-la-Mer, and Fos-sur-Mer only result in more unemployment and unhappiness. They finally end their journey on a garbage heap in the eastern section of Occitania.

Joan, Peire, and the mother are symbolic crusaders, exploring the conquered Occitanian Holy Land and seeking a place of their own in it. Each one sings a haunting refrain which encapsulates his character: Joan, the poet, the cynical fool:

> Peire a perdu la maison
> Joan a perdu la raison
> Qui est le plus malheureux
> C'est pareil pour tous les deux. (p. 28)

Peire, the giant and man of the land:

> Que pèse un homme pas grand-chose
> Que pèse un homme pas grand-chose
> Ce pays nous faisait vivre
> Maintenant il faut partir. (p. 11)

And the mother, the motivating force, an indomitable and guile-less Occitanian Mother Courage:

> Nous avons vécu. Nous vivrons.
> Nous lutterons. Nous survivrons.
> Là où un voyage se termine
> Un autre voyage commence. (p. 9)

They form an ironical Holy Family with Joan, at the play's end, sacrificing himself to the invading French army as a human target for their rifle practice (10), the mother undergoing canonization on the dump, and Peire (like the pragmatic Joseph) trying to make the best of the situation by turning the junk pile into a super flea market.

Inherent in the story of the family's exodus is a protest of the takeover of Occitania by northern French interests. In each episode of the voyage a different Occitanian problem comes to light. While working at Fos-sur-Mer, Peire witnesses the death of an anonymous immigrant worker who falls from a poorly constructed scaffolding. The scene criticizes the miserable living and working conditions of the proletariat in the newly industrialized ports of the South (11). In another condemnation of French industrialists, Peire and the mother mourn the past beauty of Saintes-Maries, whose ethereal setting is pockmarked by pollution from new factories. Several episodes depict the family's encounters with typical oppressors, in particular a bank director, a northern real estate agent, and an army commander. In two instances, Occitanian peasants recount and decry Occitania's «colonization.»

The irony which permeates the characterization and the satire which colors the denunciation of Occitania's present situation are tempered by the ritualistic superstructure of the play (12). They provide derisive flavor without diminishing the ceremonial quality of the work.

La Madone des Ordures can indeed be studied in its entirety as a conjuring up of the Occitanian warrior, with the peasant family, or «sorciers de la vie» (p. 82), administering the rite. The invocation grows in strength as the family crosses the south of France. Each member contributes to the invocation by performing a particular ritualistic function.

Joan, the poet, leads the ritual, evoking a trance-like ambiance in the opening lines, a parody of Valéry:

> Midi l'instant saisi dans un jappement
> silencieux
> Midi la mort
> Tout l'univers comme un chien qui sommeille et
> grogne dans son rêve
> Ecoutez le sommeil. (p. 7)

He blesses the audience, rendering them participants in his magic:

> . . . que la santé illumine les jours
> Des personnes ici présentes
> Venues pour voir et écouter
> Et qu'au moins une fois par jour
> malgré tout malgré tout
> Elles connaissent une joie profonde. (p. 9)

On his toy guitar, he personally accompanies the ceremonial dances of the mother and Peire (such as Peire's apache struggle «with the invisible enemy at his throat,» and the mother's fecundity waltz), and he also directs a host of secondary players. In addition, he guards the family's «sacred relics»: a doll's house, puppets, and the all-important *deux-chevaux*.

Joan is not only ritual leader but also mystic medium and sacrificial victim. From the beginning of the play, he insists he is not Joan, but Ramon VI, the Toulousan Count who, in the thirteenth century, betrayed his religious heritage by seeking and receiving absolution from the Pope. The humiliating absolution did not, however, prevent his lands from falling to the King, who annexed them along with the greater part of Languedoc. To exorcise Ramon's shame and thus give dignity back to the Occitanian people, Joan calls into himself the Count's spirit. He reenacts Ramon's penance on the steps of the Cathedral of Saint Gilles.

In the final act, Joan gives his life so that the Occitanian rebel can be born:

J'ai signé un contrat avec les militaires
Pour servir de cible vivante

. . . .
Homme-cible, homme-soleil
Vous allez voir ce beau feu d'artifice
Et moi, au centre, illuminé
Le porteur de la guérilla (pp. 96-97)

Incarnating the legendary Provençal sorceress, Tavern, the «sorcière rouge» (p. 100), Joan dies in order to prepare the Occitanian revolt.

Peire also utilizes a medium's skill to conjure up the spirits of the giants of the Crau:

Quelle est la force endormie dans le sol
Qui monte quand je frappe
Et qui me traverse le corps
Je me sens pris dans une voix
Barbare et rocailleuse (p. 73)

His second sight allows him to predict the formation of a revolutionary mass which will march against the foreigners who govern the land. Peire is the only one of the family who is capable of personally avenging his Occitanian ancestors. He keeps his herculean powers in readiness for the revolutionary call.

While Peire embodies physical strength and Joan spiritual inspiration, the mother incarnates the life force. Mythological animals dance a round in her honor, sending her on the voyage across Occitania under the protection of the fertility god («le soleil-taureau»), and praying that the future change «la vie en vie et non en mort» (p. 18). She will not, however, bear out of her own womb the revolutionary leader. Her ritual marriage with the spirits of the sea confirms her spiritual motherhood. Rather than procreate, she will encourage and watch over those who do:

Je salue le petit-fils à naître
Qui mordra dans la liberté

. . . .
Il faut un fils
Il faut un fils (p. 60)

At the end of the play, she assumes the posture and the purpose of a Renaissance Madonna. When a group of young Occitanians comes to praise her, she replies to their solemn litany with a joyous faith in the future: «La vie est belle et tu chantes / Tu ris tu remontes la pente» (p. 110). Crowned at the summit of her kingdom, the garbage heap, she smiles down upon the celebrants, investing them with her own vitality so that they may be able to carry out the revolution.

The revolutionary hero is still unborn when the play ends. The family has prepared his coming forth without engaging in the revolution themselves. Indeed, they survive their adventure across France by singing in the streets, not by revolting. Settled on top of the refuse bins, the mother sees her future in establishing a «théâtre de rue» (p. 108). She will triumph over the junk pile by transcending it in a revolutionary cry.

The active Occitanian revolutionary must emerge outside the theatrical framework. The invocation which informs the play is extended to the spectators. Having sown the essential seeds in the audience, Benedetto once again expects it to complete the revolutionary process.

Ritual is clearly the dominant formal element in Benedetto's theater. Ceremonial scenes, whether of pagan or Christian inspiration, predominate in all his plays. Ritual sequences determine the tone. Like ritual, Benedetto's theater relies heavily on signs and symbols. He uses allegorical figures, symbolic color schemes, and stylized costumes. He also regularly employs wooden puppets, inflated dolls, and cardboard dummies. The presence of a chorus also contributes to the ritual aspect of his plays. In the three examined here, a chorus chants replies, intones prayers, performs ceremonial dances and musical accompaniments.

The audience participates in the ritual both psychologically, through the direct address technique of the actors and through symbolic spectators, and physically, through the scenic structure or, occasionally, through actual physical activity. In all of Benedetto's works, the public surrounds the players. Often, as in the case of M. Dupont in Le Petit Train de M. Kamodé, the actors emerge from and take their place in the audience.

In addition, the language of Benedetto's plays is ceremonious, bearing no resemblance to everyday dialogue. In fact, he minimizes dialogue in favor of ritualistic verse forms: litany, incantation, trance speaking, and verbal rounds. Often his use of verse seems only a vehicle for the pounding rhythm which characterizes his plays, as if this intense rhythm, much more than imagery or metaphor, embodies his political fury. Yet he is also capable of producing subtle and sensual lines, especially when writing about natural phenomena or portraying affection. His sensitivity to poetic form greatly influences the scenic images which he strings together like words of a poem.

Finally, the overall structure of each work is ritualistic: *Le Petit Train de M. Kamodé*—a rite of passage, *La Madone des Ordures*—an invocation, and *Napalm*—an exorcism. For Benedetto, theater in itself is a rite and he is the ritual leader. Seeing him perform, alternately gracefully directing the dancing and furiously stamping around the stage beating out the rhythm of the words, one must agree with Emile Copferman that «Benedetto parmi ses amis est maître d'œuvre. Il est présent, un et multiple» (13).

He not only considers himself a revolutionary *meneur de jeu*, but also writes this role into all of his plays. In each, there is a character who introduces the action to the audience, entices it to join in the play's movement, and communicates the revolutionary message. In the unfinished text of *Les Incarcérées*, a kind of communion celebration with the effigy of Gabrielle Russier (14) as host, the character «Qui suis-je» explains this function:

Je suis le maître des rites, le maître des cérémonies, l'annonceur, le sorcier, le mage, le gourou, l'introducteur, le récitant, le coryphée, le meneur de jeu, l'intercesseur, aussi et l'ordinateur des pompes funèbres, le croquemort, le vénérable, le parleur, le moine, celui qui devrait avoir un nom qui n'en a pas, le régisseur, le célébrant entouré des ministres de culte théâtral, le mystagogue pour vous introduire aux mystères de la représentation, l'explicateur, le prêtre et quoi encore (15).

While Peuple and Joan, respectively, perform this role in *Le Petit Train de M. Kamodé* and *La Madone des Ordures*, the Vietnamese players, in an unusual variation, collectively fulfill it in *Napalm*.

Ultimately, each of Benedetto's plays is the same ritual. In all three, *Napalm, Le Petit Train de M. Kamodé,* and *La Madone des Ordures,* Benedetto, the revolutionary *meneur de jeu,* leads the audience through recognition of a political problem to the threshold of political action. He calls on the spectators to become revolutionary agents. The invocation rite is, therefore, fundamental to each of Benedetto's creations. Harmonizing form and content, *La Madone des Ordures* is its most successful realization.

In his insistent use of ritual, Benedetto follows his spiritual mentors, Antonin Artaud and Jean Genet (16). Long before Benedetto, Artaud called for spatial poetry, hieroglyphic figures, cries, and chants. Genet similarly demanded a theater of incantation, multiple symbols, and audience participation.

However, unlike Benedetto, Genet and Artaud reject partisan politics as dramatic motivation. By their use of ritual both artists wish to transcend social and economic conditioning. They therefore ignore one of the tenets of Marxism that most inspires Benedetto.

Like his other master, Brecht, Benedetto aims at liberating the man exploited by the capitalist system. By his choice of subjects, he places his works in a definite social and historical context. In addition, he anchors his rituals to the present by combining archetypes with contemporary metaphors, such as the Madonna of the Garbage Pile. He also undermines ritual's inherent cathartic effect by distancing his spectators. In each production, the naïveté of the ritualistic eclecticism, the actors' sense of humor towards their roles, and the obvious lack of theatrical polish puncture the ceremonial solemnity. When criticized for a dearth of professionalism, Benedetto retorts:

Si on doit faire appel à des spécialistes, à des gens qui savent bien articuler, bien marcher, etc., pour faire un théâtre révolutionnaire, il y a de fortes chances pour qu'on ne fasse qu'un théâtre bourgeois ayant un message révolutionnaire (17).

By dislocating the ritual form, Benedetto requires the audience to confront intellectually the political problems he presents.

Despite this political commitment, Benedetto fully recognizes

the limits of the direct political effectiveness of theater. Again
and again, by the nature of the invocation rite, he establishes the
frontier betweeen dramatic persuasion and political activism.
Even though he utilizes Brechtian distanciation, he can do no
more than prevent a premature catharsis. As he suggests in the
auto-criticism incorporated into each play, theater can titillate,
excite, give the spectators a certain political consciousness, and
direct them towards revolutionary action. The rest is up to
them.

Yet he counters his pessimistic view of political effectiveness
with an unequivocal support of the psychologically liberating
force of ritual theater. In this, he rejoins Artaud and Genet. According to Benedetto, ritual frees the spectator's imagination,
allowing him to be able to consider a different reality. Therefore, even if Peuple and Dupont know they have only «theatri-
cally vanquished» M. Kamodé, in *Le Petit Train de M. Kamodé*
Peuple acknowledges that «Ça fait [quand même] du bien»
(p. 103). Their triumph, even if fictional, provides a vision of
what life would be like without capitalism.

Ritual form permits Benedetto himself to embrace a revolutionary act; for by doubling reality with a poetic language of
signs and symbols, he concretizes his own freedom to break away
from accepted conceits. By further interpreting «ritual» as he
chooses, ignoring its precious and otherworldly aspect, he can
manifest his mocking disapproval of «Kultur.»

Finally, for Benedetto, the poetry which fleshes out his rituals and «revolution» are the same phenomenon. When questioned
about the ritual form of his 1968 play, *Zone Rouge*, he thus answers:

C'est un peu pour cette raison, d'honnêteté, que nous nous efforçons de
plus en plus, d'abandonner le terrain trop souvent stérile de la polémique
pour nous en tenir . . . à la poésie, pas en tour d'ivoire. Car vous le savez,
peut-être: Poésie et Révolution sont une seule et même chose. Ne serait-ce
que parce que chacune ne peut être vraiment faite que par tous (18).

Both poetry and revolution cast off spiritual shackles and celebrate life (19). No wonder, then, that the revolutionary *meneurs
de jeu*, Peuple and Joan, are poets and that their lyricism is

much more heady and vital than the verse of the other characters. Messiahs of a new order, they give hope and regenerative power.

Benedetto's combination of political commitment and ritual structure recalls Peter Brook's 1965 production of Peter Weiss' play *Marat/Sade*, itself often cited as a prime example of the contemporary synthesis of Artaud and Brecht (20). Benedetto proclaims his admiration for this production in his 1966 theater manifesto by rendering theatrical homage only to Weiss and Brook.

In the Brook production the dramatic conflict is carefully balanced between the revolutionary Marat and the *révolté* de Sade, permitting the audience to decide for itself (if at all) who is right. In Benedetto's plays, there is no question of decision as he removes all conflict, replacing it with a fascinating and original dramatic tension. For, in fact, if in all his plays the Marxist political viewpoint dominates, he nevertheless opposes the action implicit in this viewpoint to the utopia of the poetic ritual, with its inherent anarchy and suspension of action. Benedetto's revolutionary theater, as double-barrelled as he would have it, therefore presents the paradox of the Marxist who, while striving for the political liberation of the historical man, resorts to ahistorical means to liberate him psychologically. His theater is nourished by centuries-old Occidental myths and combines elements of pagan and Christian ritual with the philosphy of Jesus, Marx, Mao, and Rosa Luxembourg. His metaphors not only embody a political collective consciousness but also an archetypal collective unconscious. Although the political repercussions of such a paradox are uncertain, this combination produces a highly original dramatic result.

Chapter VI

THEATRE POPULAIRE DE LORRAINE
REGIONAL THEATER*

Le nouveau théâtre sera le fait d'équipes permanentes de professionels du spectacle, travaillant pour un public déterminé, vivant en symbiose avec une population, partageant sa vie et ses luttes, militant à la fois pour une transformation révolutionnaire de la société et pour la défense de leur profession.

Jacques Kraemer, «Notre expérience: Théâtre populaire de Lorraine,» *Travail Théâtral*, No. 8 (July-Sept. 1972), p. 71.

With these words Jacques Kraemer, director of the Théâtre Populaire de Lorraine, both defines his conception of «new theater» and describes his company. The Théâtre Populaire de Lorraine produces drama specifically for and about the inhabitants of Lorraine. In the spirit of popular theater, it reaches the nonpublic; in the spirit of political theater, it contests the status quo. It works in the tradition of what Peter Brook calls «rough theater,» spectacle which has a socially liberating role, by nature «anti-authoritarian, anti-traditional, anti-pomp, anti-pretense» (1).

The working class and lower middle class depend on the region's iron and steel industry. They are now facing a severe economic crisis, as the principal metallurgical companies desert Lorraine for the more profitable mines of Africa (2). By espousing the working-class cause in their dramatic examination of this crisis, the Théâtre Populaire de Lorraine, as Kraemer says, «shares the population's struggles,» and therefore arouses a theatrical interest in people who have previously had little dramatic experience.

This dual political and popular inspiration has characterized the troupe since its beginning. Kraemer, who in the late 1950's went to Paris with plans of becoming a second Gérard Philipe, became instead a disciple of Roger Planchon. The latter's dedication to both the theories of Bertolt Brecht and the people of his native Ardèche, encouraged Kraemer to return to his own region where theatrical activities were limited to operatic touring companies and a children's theater. In 1963, back in Metz, Kraemer established a ten-member company, organized as a workers' co-operative, whose stated goals were first «récréer les spectateurs,» awakening their critical faculties to the social and economic situation of Lorraine and secondly «établir un contact réel avec [le] public» (3), encouraging the population to go to the theater and participate in the T.P.L.'s extra-theatrical activities.

To alert the public to the political and economic injustices of the capitalist system, the T.P.L. chose to present classical and modern works rich in social criticism, concentrating especially on Molière, Marivaux, Brecht, and Adamov. Quoting Brecht in its first manifesto, the troupe explained the subversive intent of its repertoire:

S'opposant au fleuve [elle] sera la rectification du fleuve, s'opposant à l'arbre fruitier [elle] en sera la greffe; s'attaquant au mouvement, elle sera la construction de véhicules qui roulent, naviguent ou volent; s'attaquant à la société, elle sera la transformation de la société (4).

To contact the public it established an extensive information system, giving skits and lectures in high schools and at meetings of *les comités d'entreprises* (social and cultural committees) of the local unions. The actors held debates after their performances and recruited interested spectators to handle the troupe's publicity. They charged minimal prices (5), distributed a certain number of free tickets to their plays, and organized cultural evenings for the workers. Finally, their play programs are not the typical glossy homage to the actors, but analyses and explanations of their productions. Both through these activities and in its choice of repertoire the T.P.L. followed the methods of Jean Vilar at the Théâtre National Populaire de Paris.

However, unlike the liberal Parisian climate which encouraged the Théâtre National Populaire's early activities, the conservative administration of Metz balked at the T.P.L.'s first performance. Its interpretation of Adamov's *Paolo Paoli* earned the epithets of «partisan et adversif» (6). The play's sardonic condemnation of military-industrial coercion during «the Great War» prompted the city's military governor to retreat in a fury at intermission. From that moment to the present, the T.P.L. has undergone financial crises with no fixed guarantee of aid. The company's early years, 1964-1968, were therefore characterized by exhausting theatrical activity both in Metz and on tour in the Lorraine region to supplement the meager subsidies doled out by conservative municipal governments. Nevertheless, by 1968, having avoided an all-out confrontation with the regional powers in authority, the company had firmly implanted itself in Lorraine and acquired a large following.

The events of May '68 radicalized its political position and made the T.P.L. dissatisfied with theater which only treated the region's problems by allusion. During the May strikes, the actors discontinued their tour of Corneille's *Le Menteur* in order to present two agit-prop spectacles in occupied Lorraine factories. As for so many other young performers in this period, this was their first and fateful encounter with a massive working-class audience. Their successes assured them of the feasibility of a theater geared both in subject matter and in presentation to a working-class public.

No longer content with the repertoire and the methods of

Jean Vilar at the T.N.P. or Roger Planchon at Villeurbanne, the Théâtre Populaire de Lorraine decided to produce theater directly dealing with the economic and social situation of the region. As no such texts existed, the troupe set about writing its own. Its first original work, the 1969 production of *Splendeur et misère de Minette la bonne Lorraine*, according to Kraemer, «a affirmé la personnalité de la troupe» (7), for with this production the members adopted a creative method which they continue to use today.

The T.P.L. practices a collective dramaturgy in which Kraemer writes the texts on a subject agreed to by all the members. The actors and technicians work out choreography, set design, and even textual modifications during rehearsals. In this manner, in addition to *Splendeur et misère de Minette la bonne Lorraine*, they have produced six other major plays since 1968: *La Liquidation de M. Joseph K* (1971), *Les Immigrés* (1972), *La Farce du Graully* (1973), *Le Retour du Graully* (1974), *Noëlle de Joie* (1975), and *L'Histoire de l'Oncle Jakob* (1976).

All seven of these plays share a common Marxist ideology and indict not only specific regional injustices but also the larger capitalist system. The collusion of religious and other charitable organizations with powerful capitalists, the government-industrial complex, the psychological manipulation of workers and their corresponding economic exploitation recur in all; and the brain-washing techniques of mass media, especially television, are virulently attacked.

In *Splendeur et misère de Minette la bonne Lorraine*, for example, the troupe censures the French government's control over national networks. M. Joseph, an iron magnate and the villain of the play, appeases a dissatisfied worker with the gift of a television set. To his subordinate's alarmed response: «La télé y a pas de risques?» he replies, «T'inquiète pas, naïf, le Corse [the allegorical figure representing the government] contrôle les trois chaînes» (p. 58).

Because of its opposition to capitalism's use of communication to further its own ends, the T.P.L. also rails against official (capitalist) theater. The grotesque M. Joseph employs the words of «a playwright, glorified by the Académie Française,» to explain his strong-arm philosophy:

Le monde se divise en deux catégories: quelques lions exceptionnels qui
ont pour mission de chasser la gazelle et qui—c'est justice—se taillent dans le
festin la principale part, et les autres—une immensité d'imbéciles—qui sont
comme des chacals affamés et qui n'ont droit qu'aux miettes.» (p. 23)

In the downfall of «Josy K, the singing streetsweeper,» protagonist of *La Liquidation de M. Joseph K*, the troupe ironically
comments on the entertainer's subjection to planned obsoles-
cence in the consumer society. Joseph K's ruin also parodies the
officially consecrated theater of the absurd. Stuffed into a garbage pail at the end of the play, Joseph K has only his material
refuge in common with Samuel Beckett's Nag and Nell (*End-
game*). While they cannot escape a metaphysical void, Joseph K
is a captive of the capitalist system.

Of all the T.P.L.'s post-1968 plays, the first, *Splendeur et misère de Minette la bonne Lorraine*, which denounces the region's
iron trusts, comes closest both to real political muckraking and
to touching the working-class public. This results not only from
the nature of the play, but also from the conditions under which
it was produced, for the play is both keystone and culmination
of a much larger theatrical endeavor, «L'Opération Minette.»

The events of May '68 proved to the company that popular
theater should not merely function by attracting the non-public
but must also go out to it:

Il s'agit d'aller toucher le public là où il se trouve avec des spectacles du
plus haut niveau artistique et susceptibles de concerner ce public populaire
dans ses préoccupations vécues (8).

«Opération Minette,» therefore, took the form of a theatrical
crusade, with the Théâtre Populaire de Lorraine, financed by
workers' organizations and popular associations, traveling to fifteen different mining towns in Lorraine in the spring of 1969.
In each town, the actors provided a week of cultural animation
consisting of poetry readings, lectures, and short skits on the history of mining in Lorraine, the working conditions in the metallurgical industry, and the machinations of the iron trusts.

One of its two thirty-minute warm-up skits, *Parade pour Mi-*

nette, shows how the troupe prepared the mining audience for the full-length play to be performed at the end of the week. To build up public interest in theater, the T.P.L. made the sketch as meaningful as possible by basing it on metallurgical history and literature. A chorus and the two main characters, a narrator and Minette, the personification of Lorraine's low-grade iron ore, recite authentic poems, chronicles and songs, and comment on Lorraine's iron industry.

Performed in the streets or at union meetings, *Parade pour Minette* combines a glorification of the mining profession, an exposé of exploitation, and a call to arms. Mining is given a special magic, as, for example, in the recitation of the prose poem written by the miner Pierre Hemp:

> L'aciérie est comme le ciel. La nuit l'embellit.
> Du sol jusqu'au gueulard des hauts-fourneaux, tout est brasier.
> Sur ces flammes du travail du feu, les astres pâlissent. (p. 3)

Even the metaphorical Minette, whose name means both a young flirtatious girl and a low-grade ore, fascinates and excites.

But interspersed with the positive poetic description in increasing number are items which emphasize the miners' hardships. One such is the oppressive Vosges mining regulations of 1721: «Pour le logement . . . un lit servira pour quatre ouvriers. Sur les quatre ouvriers il y en aura toujours deux sur les travaux et deux au repos. Le lit sera donc toujours occupé» (p. 11). Another is Victor Hugo's melodramatic portrait of the miner in *Aubin*:

Le mineur c'est le nègre. Hélas oui. Dans la mine, on descend, on descend. On sue, on gèle, on tousse, on a chaud, on a froid. La mort fait un grand bruit quand tout à coup elle entre, c'est comme le tonnerre (p. 15).

The final item, taken from Boris Vian's *L'Ecume des jours*, chastizes the miners' resignation. Vian's engaging honeymooners, Chloé and Colin, quip about the miners' obtuseness in accepting their outrageous working conditions. At this point in the performance, the actors turn to the audience and ask, «Les mineurs sont-ils aussi bêtes que le croient les gentils personnages de Boris Vian? Sont-ils incapables de s'organiser?» (p. 20). The audience is urged to respond to the provocation by joining the actors in singing the militant 1963 «Miners' Hymn.»

Parade pour Minette, in the manner of agit-prop skits, works directly on the miners' emotions. It engenders an enthusiasm for theater by portraying the miner as a hero and transposing his preoccupations into drama. And by introducing Minette, the protagonist of both the montage and the full-length play, the warm-up sketch induces the audience to follow her story in the later production.

Whereas *Parade pour Minette* raises the audience's ire against the practices of the iron trusts in general, *Splendeur et misère de Minette la bonne Lorraine* directs this anger against specific individuals and condemns the actual situation of the iron industry in Lorraine. The lexicon of the play, published in the text and in the program notes, plainly identifies the fictional characters and imaginary locations as living persons, existing enterprises, and real sites. We read that the characters, «les truands de la vallée,» represent the major industrialists of the region: De Wendel, Usinor, Sidelor, and Lorraine-Escaut: «Les quatre trusts qui en 1965 contrôlaient la quasi totalité des mines de fer et de la sidérurgie françaises» (p. 7). «Le Château,» the gangsters' base of operations, is identified as «la résidence de la famille de Wendel à Hayange (Moselle)» (p. 8). In addition, the technical terms and mining processes included in the lexicon are invested with a critical dimension. In the entry on *enrichissement*, for example, the process is not only defined but also commented on:

Procédé qui consiste à augmenter la teneur du minerai. On connaît entre autres le procédé du flottage, celui de la lévigation et du tirage électromagnétique. *Les usines d'enrichissement sont peu nombreuses en Lorraine.* (p. 8)

The commentary subtly berates the iron industry for refusing to improve Lorraine's iron ore.

The action of the play parallels the metallurgical history of the region and depicts the current crisis in the form of an allegorical satire. As such, the play functions on two levels. On one, that of reality, the play recounts the discovery of the low-grade Lorraine iron ore, called «minette» by the inhabitants of Lorraine, a pejorative term for both mine and mineral. The story traces the ore's exploitation by the major iron trusts and, finally, its rejection in favor of richer foreign lodes. The subplot, on this level, deals with the government's relation to industry.

The other, the fictional level, is an underworld story of a sexy teenager, a «minette,» who is discovered by the gangster M. Joseph, head of a major prostitution ring. In the first part of the play, he uses her attributes and turns her into a prostitute to increase his power and gain control over the other mob chiefs, M. Roger and M. Tim. In the second part, however, he discovers that she is not as profitable as the foreign «minettes» and has her murdered. Throughout both parts, the collusion between the Valley gangsters and the Parisian protection racket, «la bande de Pigalle,» complicates Joseph's decisions, forming the subplot.

The French government's refusal to nationalize the iron mines is attacked in the play under the alias of «pigallisation étatique.» Both the character representing the head of state (le Corse) and the Valley gangsters tremble at the thought of it:

La pratique de la pigallisation étatique—ce mot me fait frémir—c'est la loi de la jungle, le retour au Bas-Empire romain, à l'Egypte des pharaons, au temps des Incas, des sauvages, des primitifs. (p. 59)

Instead of *pigallisation,* the gangsters prefer to consolidate and move their operations out of Lorraine: «Notre supermaison des faubourgs de Marseille est en route. Il faudrait liquider progressivement nos maisons de la vallée» (p. 50). The real-life iron magnates have taken precisely the same action.

These iron bosses are lampooned in the play through the grotesque portrayal of the gangsters, M. Joseph, M. Roger, and M. Timothée, who swagger about the stage imitating gangster language and gestures. Whenever this façade crumbles, they rush about, bumping into each other, taking pratfalls, and chattering nonsensically. Despite their innocuous aspect, they heedlessly ravage the land they control and destroy the people around them.

The use of allegorical satire is hardly a new theatrical technique. Brecht employs it in his play *The Resistible Rise of Arturo Ui,* to which *Splendeur et misère de Minette la bonne Lorraine* owes both the inspiration for its milieu and its style. In *Arturo*

Ui, Hitler's rise to power in Germany and his invasion of Austria are satirized as a gangster's takeover of the cauliflower trusts in Chicago and its suburb, Cicero. The Parisian painter and playwright Rezvani also uses allegorical satire in his 1972 play *Capitaine Schelle, Capitaine Eçço*, which depicts the end of the capitalist world. A luxury tanker, captained by Satyros Schelle and Sosso Eçço, accompanied by their respective wives, Eureka and Koukie, «the widow of Président JoJo,» and mistresses, Généria Motors and la Cavalcantopoulos, goes adrift when their children desert the ship. The anthropomorphic crude oil, piped out of an underdeveloped nation and stored in the hold, then revolts, hangs the passengers, and captures the ship. In the plays of both Brecht and Rezvani, the «real world» remains outside the confines of the play. The actual subject must be grasped by making an intellectual leap between the allegorical figures and their real-life equivalents (9).

In the T.P.L.'s plays, however, such an effort is unnecessary because signs from both the world of mining and its allegorical transposition, the prostitution ring, are contained within the play's structure. The double meaning of the word «minette» makes possible a constant shifting back and forth from references to prostitution to mining concerns. At the beginning of each scene of the play, a newsboy runs on stage crying out the headlines of two newspapers: *Spécial Scandale* (slanted toward the prostitution element in the play) and *Vallée-Magazine* (geared to its mining aspect). Both papers, while maintaining the duality of Minette's story, use it for their own purposes. *Spécial Scandale*, a tabloid, romanticizes M. Joseph's initial interest in Minette: «Bouleversant! Une idylle se noue entre Jo et une jeune fille pauvre,» while *Vallée-Magazine*, a trust-controlled daily, extolls the benefits of exploiting Minette: «Dans le milieu le plus estimable, on affirme que Minette assurera la grandeur de la vallée» (p. 13). In the action of the play, the visual imagery, behavior of the characters, constant double-entendres, and wordplay carry out the duality.

A representative scene (scene 3) demonstrates this dualism. M. Joseph's gang, following his orders, kidnaps Minette and brings her to the château. They are armed with machine guns (gangland prostitution) but manipulate the recalcitrant Minette with metallurgical instruments (mining world). Théo, Joseph's flunky, responds, «La demoiselle ne s'est pas montrée très compréhensive» (p. 23). (Double-entendre: Minette refuses to join Jo's prostitutes. The iron ore of Lorraine is not easily mined.) Joseph, therefore, calls in his technicians to «évaluer les possibilités de cette petite» (p. 24). (Double-entendre: her value as an iron ore, her attraction as a prostitute.) The technician attempts a series of experiments to improve her quality but concludes, «Ce bas-produit n'est pas commercialisable. Vous ne pouvez jamais en faire une grande cocotte.» To which M. Joseph responds, «Eh bien! J'en ferai une Minette» (p. 28). (Word-play: Minette = low-grade ore and second-rate whore.) The scene ends with Doctor Frensch, «Doc pour les intimes» (p. 30), plying Minette with whiskey (prostitution) and the Thomas pill (mining–a process discovered by Thomas Gilchrist used to enrich iron ore).

Although this combination of signs makes the censure of the iron trusts easily decipherable, the Théâtre Populaire de Lorraine does not depend uniquely on allegorical satire to rally the mining audience to the anti-trust cause. There are more direct attempts to prompt the workers to action. In the second half of *Splendeur et misère de Minette la bonne Lorraine,* the shifting focus from M. Joseph's exploitation of Minette to his exploitation of the workers barely veils reality in allegorical terms. The workers, «les familles de la Vallée,» characterized in the first half as apathetic employees in M. Joseph's «maison,» become crucial to the action of the play even though they are never seen on stage. Their demands force M. Joseph momentarily to lose control of the situation: «Tu sais bien, Tim, que quand les familles disent 'les patrons peuvent payer,' elles ont raison» (p. 111). Indeed, despite the gangsters' final triumph with the murder of Minette, the play ends on a warning note from «le Corse»: «Attention, quelque part dans le monde–truands vaincus par familles–attention» (p. 115). The tragedy of Minette's assassination is therefore balanced by the possibility of future action by the workers' movement in Lorraine.

The repercussions from «Opération Minette» provide vivid proof of its political efficacy. The controlling interest in the iron mines applied enough pressure on the O.R.T.F. (Office de Radiodiffusion Télévision Française) to stop televised reports of the project, and persuaded one of the two main newspapers of Lorraine, *L'Est Républicain,* to black out all coverage. After a second tour of *Minette* in 1970, the Metz municipality cancelled the company's subsidies and withdrew its theater.

The mining public's response to this introduction to theater is no less revealing. Nicole Zand reports in *Le Monde*: «Dans les villes où le T.P.L. réunissait ordinairement cinquante spectateurs, les salles furent pleines à craquer» (10). In fact, in 1969, *Splendeur et misère de Minette la bonne Lorraine* was seen by nearly 11,000 spectators, 80% of them workers who had never before been to the theater. Much later, when interviewed in a special 1970 television program on the problems of young theater, one of these spectators summed up what he had learned from «Opération Minette»: «Il ne suffit pas de faire venir des opéras, il faut aider les travailleurs à trouver le chemin du théâtre, les intéresser afin qu'ils puissent se reconnaître dans ce qui est joué» (11). While having their political consciousness pricked, the working-class public who experienced «Opération Minette» discovered the relevance of theater to their lives.

In its second post-68 production, *La Liquidation de M. Joseph K,* the Théâtre Populaire de Lorraine turned to another problem threatening the population of Lorraine: economic liquidation. Although neither naming names nor pointing a finger at a specific organization, the T.P.L. once again indicts the regional iron trusts, for the working and lower middle classes of the region face the possibility of bankruptcy from the pull-out of the iron industry. Furthermore, at the time of the play's creation, during the aftermath of «Opération Minette,» liquidation proceedings had just been initiated against the troupe itself (12). This fact adds a personal dimension to the story of Joseph K, a grocery store owner and symbolic victim, whose fate provides a comic parable of liquidation.

The play comprises thirty-two vignettes. In the first two, a school master and an army sergeant predict Joseph K's inevitable doom. In the succeeding scenes, a banker, a lawyer, a process server, a landlord, and a supermarket director seal it. Despite his work in the civic committee for small business, despite his labors in his own store, Joseph K cannot compete with the giant new supermarket, Gobkolos. Once liquidated, he never manages to hold another job and is bounced from the position of Gobkolos stocker to that of miner, nightwatchman, street sweeper, and finally, pop singer. He ends up in a garbage pail, consulting a computer about his future. But even the computer cannot help: «Je ne suis pas programmé à répondre à cette question» (p. 74).

At the end of the play Joseph K is still unsure of the significance of the hostile universe which surrounds him. For the spectators, however, the play is a vivid illustration of monopoly capitalism. Rather than being an absurd anti-hero, a first cousin to his Kafkean namesake, Joseph K clearly emerges as victim of both the Gobkolos (Grand Kapital) system and his own blindness. Presented as a typical schlemiel, Joseph K is uncomprehending, trod-on, and without a mind of his own. A sexy feminine voice, identical to that of a department store public address announcer, dictates his thoughts. Despite his encounter with a succession of liquidation agents, all the same in dress and manner, he remains completely ignorant of the economic forces that destroy him. Without understanding them, he can obviously never counter his economic oppression.

Like *La Liquidation de M. Joseph K*, the third major production of the Théâtre Populaire de Lorraine, *Les Immigrés*, exposes to its audience an insidious process, racial prejudice, and more specifically how this prejudice affects immigrant workers. Of the four million immigrant workers employed in France, one million work in the Lorraine region. They have unfortunately become double victims of the region's economic depression, experiencing it both privately and, as scapegoats for the indigent population's misfortune, publicly. While not forgetting to attack the iron industry which has caused the economic crisis, the play focuses on the racist ideas and attitudes entertained by all social classes. As Colette Godard remarks, «Le spectacle expose les divers aspects d'un chauvinisme ordinaire à peine méchant, rarement agressif, pas même idéologique, simplement provoqué par la méfiance et la peur» (13). Of the sixteen sketches of the play, four chide the lower middle class and working class, five censure the middle class, and five berate the upper middle class.

To write the play, the troupe returned to the research techniques used for «Opération Minette,» consulting specialists on the situation of immigrants in Lorraine and visiting foreign workers in their homes. The T.P.L. then presented the major themes which had evolved from its research in a half-hour montage before an immigrant audience. The final version of the play takes into account the immigrants' reactions and criticisms.

The form is that of the previous two plays of the T.P.L. However, while in them each sketch details part of a continuum (the history of Minette, the liquidation of Joseph K), in *Les Immigrés* every vignette examines a different aspect of prejudice. The first two debunk the mythology of the «savage native and noble white hunter» perpetrated in adventure movies of the 1940's, while others comment on such problems as the immigrants' working conditions and housing. In one skit, the Président Directeur Général of a large business employing immigrants trots around the personnel office directing his staff with a polo stick, while in another, professional philanthropists, guests of a television show on immigration, nearly kill each other vying for the most advantageous camera spot.

Characters are allowed to talk until they expose themselves. A waitress exclaims, «Je ne suis [pas] morphobe,» and then explains why she cannot allow immigrants in her café: «Ici c'est un café sélect. On ne peut pas servir tout le monde. . . . Ils peuvent toujours aller ailleurs» (p. 81). With a simple action added, the method attains the force of a fable. In one sketch the moral is that people do not apply to themselves the lessons they offer to others. A country grocer complains to a shopper that someone has stolen his chicken. The shopper accuses the immigrants of the theft: «Le vol chez eux, c'est une seconde nature» (p. 42). About to agree, the grocer notices a strange movement inside the woman's shopping bag and demands to search it. When the woman refuses, he forcibly opens it, finding, however, only her cat. The furious lady leaves in a huff promising never to return to the store and admonishing the grocer: «On ne doit pas accuser sans preuves» (p. 43).

Another sketch condemns police activity which, to divert attention from the real causes of the economic slump, incites the population against the immigrants. A frightened taxi cab driver and a waiter arrive late at night at the former's home. While painting anti-immigrant signs, the cab driver has inadvertently knocked out the commissioner of police. His friend promises to help him surmount the delicate situation in return for a favor—a cut of the police anti-immigrant campaign payroll! As the cab driver has no other recourse, he agrees: «J'en parlerai au commissaire. J'espère qu'il ne m'a pas reconnu! Enfin tu viendras avec moi. En cas, tu pourras témoigner que c'est par erreur et que je n'avais aucune mauvaise intention» (p. 90). Both this sketch and the country store vignette end with an ironic twist which fits into the general scheme of the play.

As in *Splendeur et misère de Minette la bonne Lorraine*, the satire is given an allegorical dimension. The immigrants are never mentioned as such, but called «anthropomorphes» or «l'animal aux pattes laborieuses.» By treating the foreign workers as mythical creatures, the play points out to what extent society has lost touch with reality in dealing with the immigrant situation.

The immigrants are excluded from the myriad characterizations until the final scene of the play. When one finally appears, he is not only as much a *homo sapiens* as his detractors but a far more dignified and personable man than his guignolesque boss. The latter, in a fit of paranoia, is attempting to flee from an imaginary immigrant plot to destroy him: «Ici, je ne me sens plus chez moi. Et eux, ils se sentent chez eux.» He cannot even start his car without his foreign chauffeur: «Je ne sais pas faire fonctionner cette machine sans lui» (p. 93). This final vignette, like the last scene of *Minette,* serves as a warning. The audience must not ignore the fact that immigrants have become an essential part of society (14).

The company's constant search for new ways to involve the regional public in its productions prompts a new dramatic approach in its fourth play, *La Farce du Graully.* After dramatically transposing three contemporary problems, in *La Farce du Graully* the troupe theatricalizes an ancient regional myth and imbues it with a political message.

The myth, which dates back to the fourth century A.D., tells how Saint Clement, sent by the Pope to evangelize the citizens of Lorraine, had first to win the people's confidence by freeing them from an enormous flying dragon, the Graully. To do so, he drowned the beast in the Moselle River, and consequently acquired the title of first bishop of Metz.

For centuries the Messins celebrated Saint Clement's Day by parading an effigy of the Graully through the city streets. Although the parades have long been discontinued, the story remains dear to the inhabitants of Lorraine. The Théâtre Populaire de Lorraine decided to produce its play in the streets of Metz, building as its playing area a giant replica of the dragon. Trucked from one quarter to another of the city and to the surrounding region, *La Farce du Graully*, like «Opération Minette,» went out to people who would not, through their own initiative, go to the theater.

Rather than dramatizing the myth exactly as it has been handed down, the T.P.L. turns the legend on its head to illustrate the mechanism of capitalist power. The play designates Saint Clement as villain and the people (a shoemaker and his wife) as the real heroes of the story. The action begins when four medieval players escape from the stomach of the Graully where they have been imprisoned for a thousand years. They laugh and stare at the spectators and immediately engage the street audience in the dialogue, with such questions as «Où sommes-nous?» «Quelle année c'est?» They decide, at last, to perform for their new audience the farce they were acting out when swallowed by the monster.

The farce presents the irreconcilable dilemma of Joseph and Berthe Jung. If they pay their taxes, they will starve. If they do not, they will be thrown in jail. They have only one chance to save themselves—to plead their case to the Governor. He, however, declares their effort futile, as the government is merely the agent for the real power, the Graully.

Clement arrives from Rome just in time to volunteer his aid to the Jungs. He lays a trap in their home that evening while waiting for the Graully to come in person and collect the taxes. When faced with the beast, however, he flees in terror. The Graully (actually the Governor in disguise), in a fit of victorious laughter, bumps his head, falls into the shoemaker's well and drowns. A while later, Clement discovers the floating Graully and deceitfully proclaims himself conqueror of the dragon, saint, bishop of the city and, as the old Governor has disappeared, new ruler of Metz. The jubilant Jungs then appeal to their protector to release them from their payments, but instead, he augments the sum by forty per cent!

Having decided to sell his well as a last resort, Joseph is astonished to find in it not only the Graully disguise but also the Governor's body. Understanding at last both the Governor's ruse and Clement's trickery, he puts the costume to his own use by returning it to the palace where he scares Clement into giving back the money to the people. The saint runs screaming off to Rome, chased by what he thinks to be «un revenant, un Graully fantôme» (p. 103).

This completes the play's demonstration: when power has no legitimacy because it has no basis in reality, its holders have to invent a bogeyman. Lest the spectators think themselves free of danger, the medieval players once more address the audience to warn them that the Graully comes back every thousand years and is, therefore, due to return that very moment! And, indeed, the T.P.L.'s previous play had dealt with one contemporary bogeyman, the immigrant.

The post-1968 productions of the Théâtre Populaire de Lorraine have evolved from agit-prop techniques applied to a regional worker-management conflict to parables whose comic structure indicts capitalism in a more general way (15). This evolution has come about because Kraemer feels that it is time to experiment with new techniques and to broaden the T.P.L.'s public base. In this way the T.P.L. will attract not only working and lower-middle-class spectators but also *la bonne bourgeoisie*, both to inform them of the worker's exploitation and to point out the parallels in their own lives.

The constants in the plays of the T.P.L. have, nevertheless, so far linked it to the working class of the region. In *Les Immigrés*, for example, the colors red, blue, and yellow, are those of French construction sites. They and the symbolic metal props—a wrench is a phone and a toolbox a typewriter—clearly center the immigrant problem in the worker's world. In all there are myriad references to mining and metallurgy and the troupe's theatrical language is chosen to appeal to the unsophisticated audiences of the region. Satire directs the audience's laughter to certain representative types (the big boss, the politician, the poor shopkeeper, the judge); parody and slapstick attack both the pretensions and the hypocrisy of the powerful. In their acting style, which they call «comic expressionism,» the actors borrow from the Marx Brothers and Buster Keaton, cabaret comedy, silent films, and adventure movies.

The sets are as broadly and purposefully designed as the characters. In *Splendeur et misère de Minette la bonne Lorraine*, for example, the decor of M. Joseph's château resembles the interior of a mine, underlining his use of machines for personal gain. His safe is actually a smelting furnace; his bar stools, mining benches; his executive chair, a combination of ore loader and driller. In *La Liquidation de M. Joseph K*, the gradual clearing away of all the props by the actors accompanies the realization of the moral bankruptcy of the protagonist and, moreover, represents the financial situation of the company. At the end of the play two actors, alone and out of costume, sit down disconsolately on the only remaining stage prop, a stage trunk, and wait.

The music, like the acting, draws upon contemporary popular culture (16). A musical number like «La Chanson du Graully Bouffetout» exhibits the naughtiness and vigor of popular songs such as «Alouette»:

> Le Graully bouffe les fesses
> Des filles de Metz.
> Le Graully pique mon lard
> Avec un coup de dard. (p. 89)

Moreover, while the lyrics of Joseph K's song «Sur le gros et le petit négoce» reinforce the criticism of the capitalist system, its interpretation by a writhing actor to a background of guitar and drums recalls the best of the singer Johnny Holliday's «yé yé» style:

> Il a des stocks démesurés
> à rotation accélérée

à l'appui gouvernemental
pour exonérations fiscales.
Tentaculaire Gobkolos
c'est l'ogre du petit négoce.
Tentaculaire Gobkolos
c'est l'ogre du petit négoce. (p. 52)

In drawing upon the styles of two of the most popular art forms, film and «pop,» the company seeks to incorporate the audience into the plays (17).

This is perhaps particularly needed because in none of the plays do we find a hero with whom the audience can identify. In fact, there are no sympathetic protagonists at all. As characters played by other characters, Joseph and Berthe Jung are distanced from the spectators, while Joseph K and Minette are anti-heroes, reacting like mechanized dolls directed by forces outside their ken. In addition, with the single exception of the last scene in *Les Immigrés*, no worker ever appears on stage.

It is the presence of the workers in the audience that completes the structure of the performance. The real protagonist of the plays of the T.P.L. is the audience itself. Without a hero, the spectators must draw their own conclusions from what they have seen. In understanding the lesson of the play, they are meant to see a way out of their own economic plight.

Chapter VII

THE AQUARIUM: AT WAR WITH
«LA REPUBLIQUE DES HONNETES GENS»

> —Vous avez raison! dit le sous-préfet.
> La forme du gouvernement importe peu!
> —Avec la liberté! objecta Pécuchet.
> —Un honnête homme n'en a pas besoin, répliqua Foureau.
>
> Gustave Flaubert, *Bouvard et Pécuchet,*
> *Oeuvres complètes,* II (Paris: Ed. du Seuil,
> 1964), 256.

From the privileged atmosphere of the Ecole Normale Supérieure, where the troupe started in 1963, to the hub of radical French drama, the Cartoucherie de Vincennes, where it now operates its own theater, the Théâtre de l'Aquarium has evolved into one of the leading advocates of satirical contestation and collective creation. Ungrateful progeny of the «solid middle class,» the Aquarium takes to task the *honnête homme* of the twentieth century. Its plays expose to ridicule and to reflection the oppressive social mechanisms and clichés of bourgeois society.

Originally uninterested in the political and social dimensions of theater, the student company took as its own the nick-name for the reflecting pool at the Ecole Normale where it met. The members chose to perform plays which suited the actors' abilities rather than the political climate of the times. Its early repertoire (1963-1965) therefore included *Antigone* by Anouilh, *Les Acteurs de bonne foi* by Marivaux, and several avant-garde sketches.

In 1965, under the influence of its new director, Jacques Nichet, the Aquarium became interested in modern adaptations of classics and technical experimentation. It consequently produced an adaptation of Aristophanes' *The Frogs* (1965); a choral drama, Aimé Césaire's *Et les Chiens se taisaient* (1965); a Planchon-inspired reinterpretation of Molière's *Monsieur de Pourceaugnac* (1966); and two rarely performed foreign works, Chekov's *Tatiana Repina* (1967) and Lorca's *Don Perlimpis* (1967).

Having acquired a reputation for innovative performances, the Aquarium turned in 1967 to a different creative method and a more critical social perspective. That fall it produced its first collective work, *Les Guerres picrocholines*. Adapted by several of the members from the Picrochole section of Rabelais's *Gargantua*, the play satirizes war and paternalistic governments, alluding specifically to Vietnam, Hitler, and Hiroshima. Nichet explains the contemporaneity of the Aquarium's production:

Si dans l'ensemble du roman nous avons retenu l'épisode des Guerres picro-cholines, c'est pour son actualité évidente; nous n'avons pas eu besoin de forcer le texte de Rabelais pour y trouver le thème actuel de l'escalade, es-calade militaire, mais aussi de l'homme par ses propres actes et par une na-ture qui lui échappe (1).

Les Guerres picrocholines censures both King Picrochole and Ruler Grandgousier, depicting as equally reprehensible Picro-chole's terrorism and Grandgousier's propaganda. In the Aquarium's interpretation, Grandgousier's reign, with its liberal taint, is the more insidious.

When presented in the professional setting of the Vieux Colombier, *Les Guerres picrocholines* earned the respect of the Parisian press. Gilles Sandier stated, for instance:

Ce spectacle est admirable d'intelligence, d'invention scénique et de force comique. Jamais peut-être je n'avais ressenti avec un tel sentiment de complicité bienheureuse la puissance poétique à laquelle parvient dans le délire bouffon, le rire dénonciateur de Rabelais! . . . La traduction théâtrale est magistrale! (2).

The play's success oriented the Aquarium towards further collective creation and social satire.

In its next work, *L'Héritier ou les étudiants pipés* (spring 1968), a collective adaptation of a sociological study by Bourdieu and Passeron, the Aquarium examines the inequalities of the educational system (3). Thematic improvisations led to a collective writing of the text which Jacques Nichet coordinated and edited. The plot opposes the fate of a working-class student, Armand I, to that of an upper-middle-class student, Armand II.

The play gave the Aquarium the opportunity to examine its own special student status and to accept a certain responsibility for the failure of students like Armand I. Thus the players conclude at the end of the play:

> Ainsi finit la comédie
>
> . . . .
>
> Si vous applaudissez
> Vous applaudissez l'injustice.
> Nous sommes complices (4).

As it deals with other, more universal student problems, the play also provided a degree of catharsis for the student strikers who saw it during May '68. Because of its adaptability, *L'Héritier* was performed outdoors and modified to correspond to the everchanging May events. It became a running critical commentary on the student revolt. This experience and the total impact of the May movement encouraged the troupe to renew its political commitment and reconsider its student position.

Faced with the failure of the May revolt, the Aquarium decided to perform a play about a successful revolution. At the summer 1968 Festival d'Alsace, the troupe presented Buchner's *La Mort de Danton*. It chose to concentrate on an established text before going on to new collective work. To complete the cast, the Aquarium recruited forty extra players from the local population. The actors prefaced their performances with a series of brilliant theatrical flashes (presaging the style of the Théâtre du Soleil's *1789*) which detailed the events of the French Revolution. Nichet's direction of the full-length play put special emphasis on the people's role as revolutionary hero.

Returning to collective adaptation in 1969, the troupe dramatized the episode of *Bouvard et Pécuchet* in which Flaubert recounts the effects of the 1848 Revolution on the municipal elections in the Normand town of Chavignolles. Its play, *La République des honnêtes gens*, characterized as «plus flaubertienne . . . que si Flaubert l'avait écrite» (5), was performed in May at the Ecole Normale Supérieure to coincide with parliamentary elections. Like *Les Guerres picrocholines* and *L'Héritier*, it had «dans l'actualité un écho immédiat» (6). Just as the play satirizes liberal thinkers, leftist intellectuals, and other *honnêtes gens* who ally themselves with repressive forces when the central power is threatened, so the *honnêtes gens* of France voted to maintain Gaullist control of Parliament.

Although a very successful South American tour of *Les Guerres picrocholines* (summer 1969) (7) assured its continuation as a university troupe, the Aquarium decided, in May 1970, to leave the university framework and become professional. In doing so, it followed the example of the Théâtre du Soleil and the Vincent-Jourdheuil Company which also gave up their university connections in the mid 1960's.

Becoming professional allowed the Aquarium to continue collective experimentation and political reflection on a full-time basis. It was also able to recruit trained actors to correct the technical limitations of the student members. The Aquarium's experience as a student company had, however, established its fundamental team spirit, a basic method—collective reflections on non-theatrical texts—and a firm political commitment. The student productions had tested and proven the efficacy of laughter as a weapon against social inequities.

Today, in 1976, the Aquarium is still characterized by a collective spirit and a sharply critical repertoire. Its material situation has, nevertheless, considerably changed. It can no longer expect the unconditional financial aid of the government. Only two of the original members, Jacques Nichet, director, and Bruno Genty, administrator, remain with the troupe. In all, there are sixteen participants: nine actors, four technicians, two administrators, and the director. The company is organized as a non-profit association, each member making the same salary— 1,600 francs ($400.00) per month. The troupe reaches all major decisions in common, and together not only creates the shows but also constructs the sets and insures the upkeep of the theater (8).

Since becoming professional, the Aquarium has produced four collective creations: *Les Evasions de M. Voisin* (1970), *Marchands de Ville* (1972), *Gob, ou le journal d'un homme normal* (1973), *Tu ne voleras point* (1974) and performed one «outside» piece, *Ah Q* (1975), an adaptation of a Chinese novel by Bernard Chartreux and Jean Jourdheuil. There is a marked change in the actors' collaboration from *Les Evasions de M. Voisin* to *Tu ne voleras point*. The latter, a political cabaret, consists of individual sketches created separately by two or three actors working together. *Ah Q*, a departure from their usual creative method, continues to condemn the power of the bourgeoisie as well as chastizing the resignation and apathy of the working classes. Co-produced by the new Théâtre National at Strasbourg, *Ah Q* has given the Aquarium breathing time from financial constraints to work on a collective creation about big business.

A troupe member's unsettling experience inspired the creation of *Les Evasions de M. Voisin*. The police had stopped the actor for questioning in the vicinity of Censier, a radical university center. The officers also questioned the proprietor of the café where he had just bought some cigarettes. Not only the café owner but also several other local merchants who had ignored his presence until the police came accused the young man of behaving suspiciously. These accusations exposed a frightening willingness to acquiesce to police oppression.

Jacques Nichet established the working outline for a theater piece which censures this attitude. During eight months of improvisations based on the outline (May-December 1970), four members, including Nichet, developed the dialogue. Nichet coordinated the work and edited the final text in January 1971. In a series of eighteen vignettes, the play reveals the true meaning of *honnêteté* in contemporary society, showing as theater critic Hélène Cingria noted, «les états d'âme d'un français moyen» (9).

The first scene of the play introduces M. Voisin, a contemporary man-in-the-street. For twenty years he has been the faithful accountant of the wine merchant, M. Tonneau. He is exact, efficient, prissy, pompous, narrow, repressed, and reactionary. His work is his life and the wine stock his family, and indeed, his religion:

> Bonne nuit, mes petits régiments!
> A demain, mes enfants sages!
> Quand je vois des chenapans, des zazous vadrouiller,
> Courir les rues, manifester, jeter des cailloux,
> Je pense à vous, mes doux jésus,
> Douillettement couchés dans la paille,
> Chacun à sa bonne place!

He loses his job, however, when electric calculators render it superfluous. Complete freedom awaits him; yet he is incapable of dealing with it. His *évasions* are a mockery, as he concentrates all his efforts on escaping from freedom.

Voisin's double and alter-ego, Zinzin, who emerges at the accountant's first taste of wine (scene 2), refuses to allow him to bury himself in a psychological prison. Lyrical, gay, and carefree, Zinzin annihilates Voisin's conception of work. Instead of laboring tirelessly when he entered Tonneau's service, Zinzin explains that he profited from the limitless wine supply: «Je me suis planqué dans le plus gros foudre—un foudre de tonnerre—un océan de Beaujolais calme et noir comme un lac—dont j'étais l'unique poisson et je ne suis sorti que les jours de paye.» Appealing to Voisin's repressed imagination, Zinzin convinces him to run off to the seashore where the two count grains of sand and chase swallows. Unfortunately, the *hirondelles* turn out to be *poulets* (police in argot) and Voisin, refusing to flee with Zinzin, ends up in a real prison charged with assault and battery.

Prison is a microcosm of the system he refuses to abandon

and suits Voisin very well. He is happy to expiate his crime and escape Zinzin's nefarious influence: «Je me console et me réjouis d'être seul, à l'abri de Zinzin» (scene 3). Zinzin nevertheless makes three attempts to lure Voisin to the outside world. Disguised successively as a judge, a bishop, and a famous chef, he cunningly tries to liberate Voisin through «acceptable» channels. As judge, Zinzin «de-condemns» Voisin; as bishop, he exhorts him to save himself from the sex-starved female inmates threatening to invade the cell; and as chef, he stashes him in a kitchen garbage pail destined for the town dump. Voisin resists all of Zinzin's wiles. Never long fooled by the disguises, Voisin refuses to fall into the trap of Zinzin's reverse psychology. Each time he is on the verge of being freed, he yells for the police.

The Zinzin episodes (musical farce) alternate with a series of cell-block scenes (social satire). The staging accentuates the difference between Zinzin's world and that of the prisoners by locating his domain on a platform extending into the audience. While the prisoners are confined to the stage and to their life in prison, Zinzin comes and goes as he pleases, addressing the audience when he chooses. His dress is frivolous and fanciful, but the prisoners' is somber and realistic.

While the Zinzin episodes castigate Voisin's attitude by ridiculing his refusal to listen to his better half, the cellblock scenes attack the capitalist system which Voisin's attitude helps perpetuate. Voisin shares his cell with five other prisoners: Monsieur (a pimp), Caïd (a juvenile delinquent), Lartigue (a mugger), Youssef (an Arab) (10), and Diogène (a tramp). Within the cell hierarchy, Monsieur, aided by Caïd, tyrannizes the rest. As he is in charge of the cell's laundry business, he controls the other cellmates. They accept his domination with abject admiration (Caïd), resignation (Youssef), cynicism (Diogène), or suppressed rebellion (Lartigue).

Introduced into this milieu, Voisin, although despising and fearing all of his cell-mates, subjects himself to Monsieur's rule in order to execute his «honest profession» and to reorganize the laundry business according to his competitive code:

L'Ordre, c'est une pile de linge propre, soigneusement

> rangée devant chacun de vous!
> La Justice, c'est un salaire proportionnel à la pile.
> La Pile la plus haute sera hautement rémunérée.
> La Pile moyenne, moyennement.
> La Dernière pile, bassement!
> Voilà l'ordre et la justice: du concret! (scene 10)

He succeeds in provoking Monsieur's praise, Caïd's jealousy, and Diogène's anger. The latter laments that despite being exploited by Monsieur, the others used to share the work equally. They worked together «en harmonie, chacun à son rythme naturel, s'entraidant selon la loi de la nature. On mettait tout en commun: travail et salaire» (scene 10).

Although the predominant style of the cell-block scenes is burlesque, the interaction between the prisoners is occasionally realistic. In such episodes, the action provides moments of intense psychological tension. When Voisin enters the cell, for example, the other prisoners decide to test his loyalty by staging a murder. If he calls the guard, they will know that he is an informer.

Lartigue proposes Monsieur as victim of the mock assassination. As Lartigue advances, it becomes clear that he really intends to kill Monsieur. Suspense mounts as the prisoners are caught between reality and fantasy, no longer sure whether or not Lartigue is acting. Only Monsieur's supreme confidence saves his life. He pits his will against Lartigue's and, as usual, the sole loser is Caïd.

The relationship Caïd-Monsieur recalls that between Maurice and Yeux-Verts in Genet's *Haute Surveillance*. However, unlike Yeux-Verts, Monsieur degrades the lackey Caïd continuously. In the final scenes of the play, Caïd's psychological burden of repeated humiliations causes him to assassinate Monsieur.

At rare instances even the burlesque mask which disguises the pathetic Voisin cracks. He momentarily becomes a «real» character. His first rejections of Zinzin's attempts to help him are tinged with an affecting sadness. He knows he cannot function outside a psychological and emotional jail:

> Oui, je pourrais facilement glisser par la fenêtre
> Oui je pourrais suivre Zinzin et sortir comme tout un chacun.

Mais partir où?
Dans quelle direction? (scene 5)

His lucid moments, however, decrease as the play develops. He progressively isolates himself from all human pleasure, including friendship. His final rejection of Zinzin destroys both his own liberty and that of the other prisoners, for he informs the guards of the prison break Zinzin initiates:

J'en appelle à tous les honnêtes gens de ma taille!
Avec moi, les amis!
Bouchons les issues, fermons les portes,
Bardons de fer les ouvertures!
A la garde!
Plantons partout des pierres de prison et
Pour protéger l'honnêteté triomphante
Construisons des prisons implacables!
L'honnête homme ne s'évade pas d'une prison.
IL LA CONSTRUIT. (scene 18)

Voisin follows the same course as Aimé Césaire's Prospero (*Une Tempête*): from the pathetic victim, there emerges an out-and-out fascist. At the play's end, his obsession triggers the mass execution of the other prisoners. *Honnêteté* not only keeps him in prison but requires that everyone else dwell there too.

In its second professional collective creation, *Marchands de Ville*, the Aquarium reduces its critical spectrum while intensifying its satirical bite. After denouncing the comportment and attitudes of *l'honnête homme* and, by extension, the social and political system perpetuated by him, it turns to a precise example of the system's evils—urbanization: «Nous avons . . . décidé de montrer comment une certaine rénovation signifie avant tout la reconquête du sol parisien par les classes aisées au détriment de ceux qui ne peuvent plus payer (11).

To render their criticism pertinent to France in the 1970's, the actors adopted the method of the theater-dossier. From February to June 1971, they consulted experts on the housing situation in Paris, read urbanization reports, and interviewed the populations of neighborhoods under reconstruction (12). Jacques Nichet again established the preliminary outline for the play, basing it on the documentation the troupe had gathered.

A month of improvisations on this first plan led him to modify the play's conception from that of an account of the fate of a widow and her slaughterhouse to a demonstration of the «renovation = deportation» mechanism. Four more months of improvisations, in which the actors embellished the major themes and developed personal interpretations of the play's characters, preceded the writing of the first text. In January 1972, Nichet completed the second and definitive script.

Whereas the events and characters in *Les Evasions de M. Voisin* are purely fictional, those in *Marchands de Ville* are derived from the Aquarium's research. Although the troupe disavowed the muckraking element ascribed to its work, it takes little imagination to see the similarities between the demolition of the *quartier* of Les Halles, the former central marketplace of Paris, and the destruction of Les Abattoirs de la Bidoche, the fictional setting of the play. Just as the French government is building a multi-story modern arts museum, the Plateau Beaubourg, where Les Halles once stood, Sacha, the architect of the Bidoche renovation project, builds «de la beauté, de la pure, de la purée, de la pure beauté, en plein cœur, un mu, un mu, un musée . . . un beau musée de purée» (p. 9). The troupe also pokes fun at the recently constructed Montparnasse Tower project in the delineation of the fictional high-rise apartments, «Tour Ginn Fizz, Tour Vermouth, Tour Cassis, Tour Double-Scotch, Tour on the Rock» (p. 103) (13). Finally a trio of prominent contemporary figures in scanty fictional disguises executes the play's renovation scheme: Volcan Balkany, an American-style European promoter and creator of the planned environment Parly II, appears as Volcani in the play; Jean Tibéri, the councilman from the fifth *arrondissement* of Paris as Tibéron; and Albin Chalandon, the former Ministre de l'Equipement, as the Talbin brothers.

To demonstrate the mechanism «renovation = deportation,» the play is divided into four main sequences, each one illustrating another aspect of the renovation process. The first depicts how «on fait du fric avec du fric» (p. 27) or how the rich become richer. It opens with a group of small promoters prospecting for land. Volcani, cleverer and better connected than the others, frustrates their efforts by discovering the Bidoche slaughterhouse: «Moi [je] suis capable d'imposer, ici, en trois mois, clés en main, un Paris plus Paris que Paris!» (p. 3). He too, however, is subject to the laws of the bigger fish. Under the collective thumb of his bankers, the Talbin brothers, he is forced to cede the Bidoche claim to them.

The second sequence examines the government's complicity in urbanization projects. César, Domitien, and Alexandre Talbin implement their plan to acquire all the land in the Bidoche *quartier*. As they must first buy the slaughterhouse, they contact the «Ministry of Slaughterhouses,» conveniently headed by brother Alexandre: «Messieurs, mes frères, je suis ministre. Vouvoyez-moi!» (p. 29). He cannot sell the property as it is part of the public domain, but he can «negotiate» it. If his brothers will build a few bus stops, a two-grade primary school, and a day-care center, Alexandre will award them enough land for «surfaces cocommerciales afférentes et attenantes, paparkings, souparkings, [et] bubureaux, surbubureaux et lologements extra-superstanding» (p. 37). In addition, the government will construct, at public expense, streets, gas mains, water pipes, and telephone and electric facilities to service the development.

Having «won» the government's approval, the Talbins then approach the upper-middle-class owners of the apartment buildings in the *quartier*. The owners are more than willing to sell their property for the right price. Thus when César informs them that «un fauteuil Louis XV plein de culs de pauvres, c'est plutôt du matériel déprécié!» (p. 49), they expel their tenants.

The third and longest sequence details the eviction and deportation from the *quartier* of the working and lower-middle-class tenants. For a certain fee from the landlords, the Talbins offer their help in the deportation scheme. Metamorphosed into *relogeurs*—Grimpinard (Crawly), La Décampe (the Mover), and Pisseloge (Pissen)—they apply legal means, psychological pressure, and force to counter the tenants' opposition. Those tenants who refuse to be relocated in half-finished housing projects miles away from the city center find that their toilets are mysteriously out of order, their garbage is no longer collected, and their neighborhood is suddenly dangerous.

Councilman Tibéron, the Talbins' flunky, placates the tenants with crafty but illogical arguments and political stratagems designed to destroy their united front, such as «J'ai trop souci de la personne humaine pour la traiter en bloc!» (p. 75). When the deadline for the new construction has passed, the future tenants of the Tour Vermouth cry scandal, prompting Alexandre, in his capacity as «Minister of the Slaughterhouses,» to employ the last resort—a massive spring expulsion in the name of the «public good.» The few remaining tenants no longer have the slightest possibility of halting the renovation and saving their homes.

The fourth and final sequence stages the complete destruction of the Bidoche *quartier*, accompanied by screaming sirens and grinding construction equipment. The Ginn Fizz and Vermouth Towers and the Talbin Bank rise up almost miraculously to delight the new population of corporation officials and junior executives. At the end of the sequence, exulting under a shower of money, the Talbins bring the renovation full circle around to new terrain. To Domitien's query, «Where next?», Alexandre proclaims, «Ici, naturellement» (p. 106), pointing menacingly at the audience.

The satirical and farcical elements of *Les Evasions de M. Voisin* are here tinged with a grotesque quality. The Talbin brothers, far more than M. Voisin, represent dehumanized forces. Whereas the portrait of M. Voisin (named after the typical man in the street) encompasses a degree of realism, that of César, Alexandre, and Domitien (named after atypically cruel emperors and conquerors) precludes any audience identification. The brothers speak in hammered phrases, adding extra syllables to their words to give them greater weight. In their macabre white and black makeup, wearing cothurni, stylized tuxedos, and three top hats, each one fitting over another, they resemble elegant draculas, systematically sapping their opponents' strength. The miniaturized *quartier*, represented on stage by small replicas of apartment buildings and stores, emphasizes by contrast the brothers' herculean stature. They merely carry off the unwanted structures and carry on the skyscrapers.

The music enhances the grotesque atmosphere and renders

the urbanization mechanism more immediately menacing than the law-and-order attitude of M. Voisin. In contrast with Zinzin's light song and dance numbers in *Les Evasions de M. Voisin*, the pounding rhythm and melodramatic phrasing of the recurrent piano theme in *Marchands de Ville* augment the tension. The pianist, M. Fric, suspended over the stage with his instrument, orchestrates the discovery of the slaughterhouse, the construction of the skyscrapers, and the destruction of the *quartier*. Volcani dances unwillingly to his music while the Talbins personify its rhythm and mood.

In complete contrast to the grotesque aspect are a series of naturalistic encounters with the inhabitants of the Bidoche *quartier*. These occur intermittently throughout the third sequence. While marionettes represent the tenants in the satirical sketches (to signify their manipulation by others), in the naturalistic ones an actor playing a tenant recounts his story directly to the audience. This procedure involves the public in the lives of the Talbins' victims. From its objective vantage point the audience can see through the Talbins' trickery, even when the tenants cannot.

The interrelated stories describe both the activities to save the neighborhood and the treachery of the *relogeurs*. Each tenant has a different point of view. These vary from the apathetic: «Je ne vais pas faire de la politique maintenant pour me mettre à dos mes clients, gauchers ou droitiers» (p. 67), to the militant: «Ils rénovent notre quartier! Tant mieux! Nous voulons en profiter! . . . Nous nous battrons pour notre droit à la ville» (p. 69). The dangers of a passive or «each man for himself» attitude are illustrated in the fates of the apathetic bartender, whose customers all move away, and the frightened worker, whose relocation to Trives-la-Suze necessitates a bus ride, train trip, subway excursion, and seventeen-minute walk before he arrives at his job at the Place d'Italie. The militant's tête-à-tête with the spectators informs them how to prevent or improve relocation. He explains the 1948 law: «Si on vous expulse on doit vous reloger pour le même loyer, à la même distance de votre lieu de travail. Tant qu'on ne vous propose pas ça, refusez, vous êtes dans votre droit» (p. 13). His passionate dedication to the common cause of the tenants illustrates the Aquarium's solution to the housing problem.

As in *Les Evasions de M. Voisin*, fantasy and burlesque take precedence over realism in *Marchands de Ville*. The alternation between the contrasting stylistic elements results in fascinating changes in tenor and mood. Even the self-declared enemy of political theater, *Figaro* critic J.-J. Gautier, admits the effectiveness of this technique:

> C'est mordant sans doute, mais surtout drôle. C'est symbolique, mais pas théorique ni jamais ennuyeux. C'est banal si l'on veut: la lutte des petits promoteurs contre le gros, la façon d'expulser les locataires gênants, la résistance du bataillon des charlots. . . . Mais combien cela est intelligemment conçu! Et quelle invention constante. (14)

Marchands de Ville grips the spectator emotionally and appeals to him intellectually. The combination of burlesque and realism permits the Aquarium to provide, without preaching, a serious explanation of what can be done to combat the renovation-deportation cycle.

Like *Marchands de Ville, Gob, ou le journal d'un homme normal* deals with one particular aspect of *la république des honnêtes gens*, the press. Whereas *Marchands de Ville* is based on objective analysis, *Gob* is based on the subjective relationship between the reader and his newspaper: «Comment se comporte le lecteur vis-à-vis de son journal, des mythes, des clichés, des stéréotypes, des fragments de réalité qui s'y trouvent inextricablement mêlés» (15). The play denounces both the reader who is unable to think for himself and the press which perverts the news to its own ends.

Jacques Nichet proposed as point of departure for the creation of the play an excerpt from Paul Nizan's *Les Chiens de garde* which depicts the middle-class man as living among shadows and reflections:

> Le bourgeois est un homme solitaire. Son univers est un monde abstrait de machineries, de rapports économiques, juridiques et moraux. . . . Il aperçoit seulement des ombres. Il n'est pas en situation de recevoir directement les choses du monde. . . . Il vit au milieu des reflets (16).

For a month each member improvised sketches on the «reflections» which comprise the daily news. Although fertile, the improvisations were too divergent to form the basis of a text. An actor therefore suggested that the improvisations be confined to the press' treatment of one news item, choosing as focal point the Bruay-en-Artois affair.

On April 6, 1972, in the mining town of Bruay-en-Artois, two children discovered the nude and mutilated body of sixteen-year-old Brigitte Dewevre. The corpse had been placed in an empty lot adjacent to her home in the miners' housing complex. Seven days later, Pierre Leroy, a middle-aged notary and one of the town's most prominent citizens, was arrested on suspicion of murder. The police arrested his girlfriend, Mme Monique Béghin-Mayeur, a wealthy businesswoman, two months later, accusing her of complicity in the homicide. The *juge d'instruction*, Henri Pascal, directed the investigation in order to determine whether a solid case could be made against the suspects. According to French law, such an investigation must be kept strictly secret. Nevertheless, Judge Pascal gave many interviews to curious newsmen, freely expressing his suspicions of the couple and declaring the «people's» right to his discoveries. Local and out-of-town Maoists played up the political implications of the case, accusing Leroy of a crime against the working class. Already antagonized by years of social and economic discrimination, several miners formed a local committee of «truth and justice.» They held demonstrations in front of Mme Mayeur's home, distributed a newspaper (*Pirate*) to support Judge Pascal and to prevent Leroy's liberation, and published a book on the affair (*Bruay: Dossier publique de l'affaire*). Despite these activities, both Leroy and Mayeur were eventually allowed provisional liberty and Judge Pascal was taken off the case, his superiors citing unprofessional behavior. On April 18, 1973, Jean-Pierre Flahaut, seventeen, a friend of Brigitte Dewevre's, confessed to having killed her, a confession he retracted one month later. At the time of the creation of *Gob* (December 1973) all three persons, Leroy, Mayeur, and Flahaut, remained accused of the crime (17).

The Bruay-en-Artois crime might have remained a banal *fait divers* if it had not captured the press' attention. Jean-Louis

Clavet, writing in *Politique Hebdo*, attributes the news media's fascination with the crime to the improbability of the criminal: «Un notaire, d'une part, avec tout ce qu'évoque en France cette fonction (rondeur, respectabilité, revenus confortables) et d'autre part un crime qui évoque tout sauf la vieille France notoriale» (18). Whatever the reason, for a five-month period the affair occupied the columns of publications as diverse as *Détective* and *Le Monde* (19). Reporters literally set up camp in Bruay to record and often to invent the most minute actions of the accused.

The Bruay-en-Artois affair, therefore, provided an excellent source for the Aquarium's examination of the press-reader relationship. After reading and compiling dossiers of nearly all the press releases on «Bruay-en-Artois,» the Aquarium began transposing them into dramatic scenes. As its concern was not about the scandal *per se* but about the press which reported it, the troupe not only improvised sketches based on the news items but also worked on possible reader reactions to them. Five months of improvising led to the establishment of the first outline. More than in any of the Aquarium's other creations, the *mise en scène* informed the text. Indeed, Nichet compiled the first script only a few days before the play's opening.

The final work combines a dramatic transposition of twenty press items and a portrayal of a «typical» reader's reaction to them. The publications used (and cited in the play itself) include: *France-Soir* (four articles), *Le Monde* (three articles), *Détective* and *Le Journal du dimanche* (two articles each), and *L'Express, Le Parisien libéré, Paris-Match, La Cause du peuple, L'Aurore, L'Humanité, Minute, Le Figaro*, and *Ici Paris* (one article each). Half of the items are thus gleaned from «popular» publications geared toward sensationalism, while the other half represent «liberal» (5), «left» (1), «right» (1), «far right» (1), and «far left» (1) papers.

The dramatic transposition of the news items is realized in two manners: direct quotation and analysis-synthesis. An example of direct quotation takes place when a reporter, announcing himself from *France-Soir*, interviews the Fiancée. In the play, the persons involved in the Bruay affair are called by their social category rather than by their name; thus «the Notary,» «the Judge.» The Fiancée's replies and the reporter's questions, his asides, and even the punctuation which he cites exactly duplicate an interview with Mme Mayeur in *France-Soir* (20).

The analysis-synthesis method consists of communicating the attitude and color of the news item rather than quoting it directly, although certain phrases from the article may reappear in the dialogue. The Aquarium uses this method more frequently than the other. An example of this technique is the Spencer Tracy episode. A reporter from *Le Journal du dimanche* comments:

Le juge, il me fait penser irrésistiblement à un héros du cinéma américain des années 50—peut-être même un personnage du western—vous savez bien —un Spencer Tracy, buté, acharné, solitaire, qui ne recule devant rien pour trouver la vérité.

At the conclusion of this description (a direct quote from an article in *Le Journal du dimanche*) (21), the reporter, putting on a western hat and a holster, becomes the Judge. He encourages the reader, who is present in all the sequences, to follow him in his lonely trek for justice; and the two begin a dogged march around the playing area to the background music of «Home on the Range.» They stop only to allow the reader to try on the Judge's cowboy hat. The Judge explains, «Je l'ai acheté le jour où j'ai acheté ma première étoile.»

Both techniques require a visual translation of the images evoked in the articles. In some cases the image lasts only a moment and resembles a news photo, as when three couples of the victim's parents—«Les Malheureux Parents»—*L'Express*—«Les Parents affligés»—*Paris-Match*—and «Les Douloureux Parents»—*Le Parisien libéré*—descend into the playing area and then disappear back into the wings. In others the image is developed and prolonged, as that of the «bourgeois-cannibals» described in an article from *La Cause du peuple* (22). Hiding under his bed, the reader watches a party of nineteenth-century bourgeois tear at the cadaver of the victim, orgiastically drinking her blood and writhing in pleasure on the stage floor.

Gob is the name of the reader created by the Aquarium to receive and respond to all the dramatically transposed news items.

He believes everything he hears, without reservation (*gober* in French) and absorbs others' ideas and language. Gob is thus a mere shell of a man. Like M. Voisin, he is a lower-middle-class employee—a shoe salesman. Unlike M. Voisin, who is self important (*se gobe*), Gob is unimportant. He exists only because he reads and in function of what he reads. The violence he commits is limited to his own psyche.

Gob inhabits an abstract space, that of his own reading, represented in the play by a bed enclosed in a blue, sand-covered arena. News literally descends upon him from the mountain of newspapers built up on one side of the set. Reporters, dressed as waiters and waitresses, climb down from the stacks of papers, offering their services and their goods. They shift back and forth from their roles as journalists to those of characters in their own stories.

The Aquarium singles out four categories of reader reaction to the Bruay-en-Artois affair which correspond to four ways of handling the news: narcissistic, detective, political, and heroic. When the newspapers do not render Gob impotent by drowning him in sentimentality or by assuaging his conscience with abstract terminology, they turn him into a vigilante. The play is structured according to the four categories, while the news items in each one are arranged chronologically according to the Bruay-en-Artois events. They provide a time continuum of one year within the timelessness of Gob's reading.

In the first sequence, Gob appropriates the news items, identifying with the press' interpretation of the protagonists. He is successively, the Victim, the Evil Notary, and the Notary-Scapegoat. He equates his own unhappiness with the parents' sorrow: «Moi, aussi, j'ai ma croix, chaque jour à vendre des chaussures.»

In the second he becomes a detective, striving to figure out the true character of the Notary and determine his guilt or innocence. Transported by a news article from *France-Soir* to the site of the crime, he examines over and over again the clues presented to him by two reporters. *Detective* allows him to consult «la belle et sculpturale Lulu,» a prostitute from the «sordides abîmes des quartiers de plaisir à Lille,» who knew the Notary as her client.

In the third sequence, he accepts a political interpretation of the crime only to arrive paradoxically at a final apolitical stance. Although the *Journal du dimanche* points out to him the difference between the *nantis* and *non-nantis* of Bruay-en-Artois, Gob vacillates between accepting the *Cause du peuple*'s condemnation of the bourgeoisie and *Aurore*'s presentation of the Notary as a suspect without class affiliations.

In the fourth sequence, Gob takes upon himself the burden of the just. He is compelled by «le petit juge» from *Le Journal du dimanche* to join his crusade for the truth: «J'ai besoin de toi, mon petit. Pour moi, la justice, que ce soit un ouvrier ou un roi, c'est pareil.» However, once again Gob is waylaid from a straight course by the conflicting images to which he is subjected. The Judge from *Minute* resembles an executioner from the Terror. And the original heroic judge vanishes when a reporter announces that the Notary has been released from prison.

Each of the four sequences ends with a chorus of Gob-like characters echoing the predominant viewpoint. After the first sequence, a Breughelesque tableau of cripples and blind men laments the fate of humanity. A gathering of vigilantes concludes the second sequence, with the participants planning a reign of silent terror. The finale of the third sequence comprises a group of sick men washing their hands of any involvement in the affair. And after the fourth, guardians isolate personifications of «truth» and «justice» from contamination by the masses.

In the fifth and final sequence of the play, the hollowness of all the roles imposed on and accepted by Gob is illuminated when the journalists bring him the news that he has been following the wrong suspect all the time. The reporters, having worn out the Bruay-en-Artois affair, drop it, leaving Gob to his shoes. He ends up dipping his newspaper, like a croissant, in his coffee, desperately crying out: «Si cette affaire ne vous intéresse plus, racontez-moi autre chose . . . Ayez pitié du pauvre Gob et de son âme de papier. Sans vous, par quoi est-il raccroché à l'existence?»

By including excerpts from publications which range over the entire political spectrum, the Aquarium proves its readiness to criticize the press in general and not just a segment of it:

Les comédiens-auteurs de l'Aquarium ne sont pas des militants: ils ne nous proposent pas de contre modèle d'information. Ils se contentent de mettre en question 'le grand amortisseur de l'événement': la presse (23).

Its Marxist bias does, however, color the troupe's criticism of certain papers. It satirizes the superior attitude and «we are above politics» stance of *Le Monde*, for example, by always positioning the paper's reporters at the summit of the mountain of newspapers. From there, they pompously proclaim the paper's impartiality:

Dans cette affaire, il y a d'une part l'agitation groupusculaire, d'autre part la politique. Et dans la politique, il y a d'une part la gauche, d'autre part la droite. Par souci d'objectivité *Le Monde* mesure la parole à gauche et à droite.

Le Monde motivates Gob to think in categories rather than in human terms.

The Aquarium's reluctance to criticize *La Cause du peuple*, a Maoist-oriented journal of which it approves, is also evident. After a broad satire of the *Cause du peuple*'s article on bourgeois-cannibals, the play includes an apology for the paper's overreaction. The *Cause du peuple*'s reporter concludes: «Nous les militants de *La Cause du peuple* avons peut-être dit des conneries—mais au moins on est allé là-bas sur le terrain et c'est là-bas aussi où on pouvait corriger—sur le terrain.» This is the only comment of its kind in the play (24).

More than either *Les Evasions de M. Voisin* or *Marchands de Ville, Gob ou le journal d'un homme normal* is an intellectual play. Unlike Zinzin and the tenants in the first two plays, no character in *Gob* involves the spectator in the action by direct address techniques. There are no realistic elements to appeal emotionally to the public. Furthermore, in *Gob* there is no spokesman for the Aquarium's point of view. Diogène in *Les Evasions de M. Voisin* and the militant tenant in *Marchands de Ville* propose a solution to capitalist exploitation. But in *Gob* the themes of class consciousness and united action are lost in the all-encompassing condemnation of the press. In *Gob*, the Aquarium looks at reality at an angle that invites reflection. It poses questions but does not suggest answers. By bringing to life exaggerated and oversimplified newspaper images, *Gob* allows the spectator to see for himself the way in which the press abuses the reader.

The Aquarium has evolved a method of collective analysis and composition which directly involves each member in the creative process. Until the creation of *Gob*, Jacques Nichet always wrote a preliminary outline. The structure of *Gob*, however, developed through the actors' improvisations. Thus, whereas only four members worked on the text of *Les Evasions de M. Voisin*, all of the members participated in the elaboration of *Gob*.

Despite the collaboration of the other members, Nichet's editing still gives a unified style and form to the Aquarium's work. He assures, in particular, clever dialogue and consistent characterization. Consequently, the Aquarium's scripts, especially those of *Les Evasions de M. Voisin* and *Marchands de Ville*, are more coherent than those of other collective creations. In them, there is little room for the kind of textual improvisation which can unbalance a performance.

With the increased activity of each member in the creative process, there is a corresponding growth in the importance of the *mise en scène*. The texts of *Les Evasions de M. Voisin* and, to a lesser extent, *Marchands de Ville* permit a number of interpretations in set design and choreography. However, as the text of *Gob* and its *mise en scène* were developed simultaneously, the two are inseparable. One explains and informs the other. The visual impact of the mountain of newspapers pouring into Gob's bedroom is necessary to unify his various experiences.

The evolution in creative method has also influenced the political impact of the Aquarium's productions. In *Gob*, the lack of a single directing force blurs the troupe's political bias. The members were unable to coordinate their work in time to include a spokesman for their political position. Furthermore, the production's interdependence of script and set precludes taking the play on tour. As the set was constructed within the design of the theater itself, the Aquarium cannot perform in any other playhouse. Consequently, with *Gob* the actors do not have the mobility they had in May 1968, which allowed them to perform in the street, or in spring 1972, which allowed them to take *Marchands de Ville* to various Parisian neighborhoods undergoing renovation.

The Aquarium's street experience with *Marchands de Ville*, which it performed for free approximately twenty times in support of rent strikes and tenant associations, was its only professional attempt at agit-prop theater. Although the members would like to continue this kind of activity, they find it financially impossible. Like Molière, the Aquarium has learned that to exist with the minimum of peril as a subversive agent among *les honnêtes hommes*, it must impose limits to its protest.

Chapter VIII

THE IMPACT OF CONTEMPORARY
REVOLUTIONARY THEATER

> Le réalisme politique, le seul qui serve l'humanité, doit s'o-
> rienter vers les valeurs fondamentales, mais en restant tou-
> jours un art du possible. Le théâtre n'est pas lié à de telles
> contraintes, il peut viser l'impossible. Les politiciens doi-
> vent envier les hommes du théâtre.
>
> Willy Brandt, «L'Allocution du chancelier fédéral
> sur 'théâtre et politique,'» trans. Philippe Ivernel,
> *Travail Théâtral*, No. 10 (Oct.-Jan.), p. 152.

The agony of the government-sponsored popular theater movement, witnessed even before May '68 and confirmed after the
May events, is now over. State-subsidized popular theater is
dead. In July 1972, Bertrand Poirot-Delpech proclaimed, «1972
restera une date dans l'histoire du 'théâtre populaire': celle de sa
mort. . . . Cet idéal de culture sans classe n'anime plus sérieuse-
ment aucune troupe subventionnée» (1). Not only have the *maisons de la culture* eliminated their inexpensive subscriptions,
thus abandoning the policy of attracting working and lower-
middle-class audiences to their theatrical productions, but they

have also begun to place more emphasis on sports than on theater.

Indeed, the transformation of Roger Planchon's Théâtre de la Cité into the new Théâtre National Populaire in the spring of 1972 has arrested rather than advanced popular theater. After attending the Villeurbanne-T.N.P.'s inaugural work, Poirot-Delpech ironized over the production's lack of concern for a popular public: «*Massacre à Paris*, tiré de Marlowe par Patrice Chéreau, a apporté la preuve . . . que faute d'atteindre le 'non-public' défini en 1968 à Villeurbanne même, les nouveaux maîtres du T.N.P. se souciaient peu de 'culturiser' ou seulement de divertir la petite bourgeoisie» (2). Patrice Chéreau, Planchon's co-director, has rejected his earlier attempts at a *théâtre engagé* and a *théâtre sectaire* to celebrate his baroque esthetic sense in a series of extraordinarily fastidious and costly stagings. Bogged down in administrative work, Planchon has all but renounced his attempts to create a popular and political theater.

While the appointment of Jack Lang (3) to head the ex-T.N.P., now the Théâtre National de Chaillot, raised hopes for a revitalized popular theater, his choice of repertoire belied any popular inspiration. In 1973-1974 the Théâtre National de Chaillot sponsored a series of esoteric productions based on legends and mythology, including an hermetic interpretation of *La Princesse Turandot* by the Rumanian Lucian Pintilié which featured thirteen «international» dwarves. Lang's successor, André-Louis Perinetti, has been forced to reconvert Chaillot into a theatrical garage. In 1976 Michel Guy, Secretary of State for Cultural Affairs, refused to fund its creative endeavors.

The government's flagging interest in the goals of popular theater can be linked to the politicization of the popular theater movement. Had popular theater never attempted to criticize existing structures, it would probably still be enjoying the full benefit of the coffers of the State. The governement money lavished on Planchon's and Lang's prestige productions indicates this. The government awarded 5,000,000 francs each in 1973 to the new T.N.P. and to Chaillot, but allocated a total of only 25,150,000 francs to the nineteen other decentralized companies. These sums, when compared to the 25,129,850 francs given to the Comédie-Française and the Odéon alone (4), point to the government's preference for a theater which either conserves the cultural patrimony and the cultural domination of the middle class or fosters an innocuously flashy avant-garde.

Theater critic Renée Saurel demonstrates that government policy under President Pompidou aimed to control and choke politicized popular troupes (5). She deplores the resulting sabotage of political awareness and theatrical creativity:

> Il faut être bien ignorant de la situation générale du théâtre, ou bien hypocrite, pour soutenir que le pouvoir n'a pas de politique cohérente. Elle est au contraire évidente, elle tend à l'industrialisation du théâtre, consacre la domination des technocrates et des 'intendants,' commis par l'Etat, sur les créateurs, sacrifie de plus en plus le vrai travail de création et de culture au prestige—la 'queue de paon'—national et international.

Indeed, the government's covert and overt pressure pits theater professionals against each other in an effort to retain or obtain financial help. The director Roger Blin comments:

> Ce qui se trame actuellement, c'est le décervelage et la liquidation à terme des artistes créateurs, les uns après les autres et les uns *par* les autres. L'un espèrera un an de grâce si on obtient de lui une vacherie à un collègue. Ce qu'on vous demande, c'est d'être bien sage autour de la mangeoire du ministère (6).

Directors and playwrights have begun to censor their own work to qualify for subsidies.

Perhaps the real *coup de grâce* to subsidized popular theater (doubtless the most spectacular demonstration of the government's opposition to the politicization of the movement) occurred in the spring of 1973. In an interview, Maurice Druon, Resistance hero, author of historical biographies, and newly appointed Minister of Cultural Affairs, explained his conception of his office:

> Que l'on ne compte pas non plus trop sur moi pour subventionner par préférence avec les fonds de l'Etat les expressions dites artistiques qui n'ont d'autre but que de détruire les assises et les institutions de notre société. *Les gens qui viennent à la porte de ce ministère avec une sébile dans une main et un cocktail Molotov dans l'autre devront choisir* (7).

He implied that theatrical subsidies would henceforth be determined according to the content rather than the overall quality of a troupe's work and that any project deemed subversive would be rejected.

Intellectuals, artists, actors, directors, and political opponents reacted as if Druon himself had launched the first bomb. From Jean-Louis Barrault to Marcel Achard everybody commented on Druon's attack on freedom of expression and on his scorn for creators. Barrault proclaimed that Druon had tolled «le clairon de la répression» (8). Boulevard playwright Achard, on the contrary, in a speech welcoming *Figaro* critic J.-J. Gautier into the Académie Française, typically praised Druon and criticized the entirety of young experimental, and subsidized theater (9).

The protests, which far outweighed the praise, culminated in a demonstration on May 13, 1973. The Théâtre du Soleil, the Aquarium and the Association de l'Action pour Jeune Théâtre (L'A.J.T.), the Vincent-Jourdheuil Company, and the Ensemble of Gennevilliers organized a funeral march to mourn the death of «free expression.» Dressed in black and gagged, accompanied by a forty-piece band, and following a horse-drawn hearse with the cadaver of «free expression,» some five thousand participants solemnly marched from the Bastille to the Place de la Nation.

Despite the massive publicity, the demonstration, far from effecting a change in Druon's policy statement, instead cemented his opinions. In a May 23 speech before the National Assembly (10), although he attempted to make amends for turning intellectuals and artists against him, Druon compounded his reactionary stance. He condemned bestiality, perversion, sexuality, violence, vulgarity, and, generally, anything which countered the theatrical image of a noble and matriarchal France, the «source of Western civilization.» He again showed a total indifference to the evolution of art and to the search for new means of expression, longing rather for an official, academic art and for the humanism of «le bon vieux temps.»

Druon's remarks definitely refuted those critics who had been proclaiming that art had no political dimension. His hard-line tack, however, also frightened a great many authors and directors of subsidized dramatic centers into de-emphasizing this dimension. Official theatrical conservatism waxed again, more strongly than after May '68, and without a cloud of rhetoric to hide it.

The «Druon affair» ultimately proved that both popular theater and experimental theater lie in the hands of the young, unsubsidized or marginally subsidized companies which emerged out of May '68 (11). It was indeed the Théâtre du Soleil and not the T.N.P. which organized the march for freedom of expression. Moreover, the Théâtre du Soleil and companies like it maintain the contact with workers which most subsidized theaters have stopped. The Soleil and the Aquarium, for example, regularly hold discussions with workers to gather information for their improvisations. They often perform these before a working-class audience and incorporate its criticism in their final creation. When requested, most young troupes will perform agit-prop skits for the benefit of striking workers. Benedetto makes himself and his actors available to committees of workers throughout France with whom he creates plays based on local or work-related problems.

The public flocks to the low-priced productions of the marginal companies. During the same period when the Soleil played before a total of 322,027 spectators with *1789* and *1793*, the public of all the National Theaters combined comprised only 568,000 spectators, a 50% decrease from the early 1960's (12). The Cartoucherie de Vincennes has become the real T.N.P. of the 1970's.

The post-68 popular theater has carried cultural democratization much farther than its mentor Jean Vilar. Its socialist ideal, to break the system of capitalist rapports, informs the process of theater making and the theatrical institution as well as theatrical content. The audience often participates in the creation and in the action of the play. The spectators are sometimes the play's collective hero. The public, rather than the «star,» is the focal point of a performance. The troupe members receive equal salaries and make joint decisions concerning troupe activities. No longer only performers, the actors exercise a variety of talents—directing, lighting, decorating, writing. They consider themselves very much part of society, neither haughtily isolated nor humiliatingly exiled.

The fruitful results of «socializing» the theater have even affected political playwrights such as Georges Michel and Armand Gatti. Formerly solicited by numerous subsidized popular theaters, since 1968 Michel has suffered the consequences of an unacknowledged censorship. Most of his new works are now done by provincial or amateur troupes. He has therefore joined with fifteen partners to open «La Cour des Miracles,» a cooperative theater and art center, «pour donner la parole à ceux qui ne peuvent pas, qui ne peuvent *plus* la prendre en d'autres endroits» (13). The profits from the restaurant and café which form part of the complex are used to cover theater and cinema costs. La Cour des Miracles can thus produce any controversial or experimental work without worrying about losing money.

Armand Gatti has had even worse problems programming his plays in France since 1968. He has accordingly redirected his theatrical endeavors. Convinced that he cannot bring theater to the workers, he would rather inspire the working class to create. Thus, in spring 1973, with his students from the Institut des Arts de Diffusion in Louvain, he spent several months in the Brabant, in Belgium, setting up committees of peasants and school children to write and rehearse sketches about their most urgent problem, the Common Market. At the end of May, the three thousand participants gathered together for a twenty-eight hour festival, in which nine of their skits were performed. The collective creation now practiced by Gatti, contrary to the method of the Théâtre du Soleil, eliminates the spectator. Everybody is a creator and actor.

Both Michel and Gatti have learned the merits of not being tied to the government's purse-strings. Theater critic Darko Suvin insists on the need for financial independence in the life of the theater: «If there is any future for significant theater, dramatic or other, it lies in theater groups organized on the basis of socialized self-management: run by the ensemble itself with responsible interplay with the communities from which the audiences are drawn» (14). Suvin warns that the creative element of every subsidized ensemble will eventually conflict with the bureaucracy which funds it, unless it is willing to become a museum.

Condemned to «being a success,» government-subsidized theaters dare not experiment. In 1966-1967, for example, of the sixty works produced by State-financed theaters, only four were new French creations. The Ministry of Cultural Affairs devotes a mere one-thirtieth of its budget to theatrical research (15). Even the Avignon festival, formerly a place for exchange and experimentation, has been transformed into a market for directors of *maisons de la culture*.

Because they do not depend on the government's generosity, the politicized post-68 theater companies need not worry about taking esthetic risks. More than any other aspect of this theater, it is its freedom to experiment which makes it revolutionary and valuable. The Théâtre du Soleil, the Aquarium, the Théâtre Populaire de Lorraine and André Benedetto have tried out new or forgotten forms of theater. All four have rediscovered old popular styles, such as fair theater, commedia dell'arte, and cabaret and adapted them to contemporary tastes, even creating new tastes. They have developed improvisations to a high art and reinvested the theater with a certain primitive energy which makes their productions sparkle with life. They have also studied and practiced collective creation, which, while not always satisfactory, is certainly challenging accepted ideas about creation, and, moreover, stimulating individual writers (16). Finally, they have reintroduced into the playhouse the laughter which comes from hope and not from desperation.

There is a paradox inherent in this freedom, for if their lack of government support allows these companies creative liberty, it also often condemns them to subsistence living. A marginal existence can, in turn, annul all possibility of creation. From spring 1973 to winter 1974, the members of the Théâtre du Soleil were forced to stop rehearsing and collect unemployment insurance to survive. As the men and women engaged in political theater are overwhelmingly theater professionals before they are political activists, they respond to the dilemma of subsidy or subversion, whenever they have the choice, by «taking the money and running.» They want, above all, to do theater, even if this means accepting government aid.

Nevertheless, and perhaps for the good of their consciences if not their stomachs, not very much money is forthcoming. Indeed, in March 1973, half of the members of the Commission Consultative d'Aide aux Jeunes Animateurs (the committee which awards money to young theater groups) resigned because of their frustration with the government's hostility and indifference. In 1972, they had 2,520,138 francs to distribute and eighty-five dossiers to consider. In 1973, this sum was reduced to 1,879,600 francs while the number of troupes applying for aid increased to one hundred and sixteen (17).

The obvious solution to creative freedom and full stomachs is to find another source of income besides government allocations. Box-office profit alone does not suffice as operating costs far outweigh the low admission price asked by these theater groups. Following the lead of the Italian actor and militant Dario Fo, the Théâtre du Soleil is taking a step towards financing its own productions by asking its public to co-produce them. In the Théâtre du Soleil's scheme the spectator buys an advance ticket for more money than the actual cost of entry. The surplus goes into the production. The Aquarium, too, has brought in extra money by serving meals before its political cabaret *Tu ne voleras point*. And Benedetto's troupe practices the tried but exhausting method of second jobs for the members.

The post-1968 theater is not succumbing to financial pressure. Perhaps this theater prospers in adversity for it is unquestionably the most vital theater in France today. If, in the future, it does not revolutionize society, it nevertheless will be responsible for having brought about a fertile change in theatrical practice.

NOTES

CHAPTER I

1. Peter Brook, *The Empty Space* (London: Pelican Books, 1968), p. 44.

2. In 1892, Maurice Pottecher created the first Théâtre du Peuple in his village in the Vosges, inaugurating the experience with a production of *Le Médecin malgré lui* in the local dialect. Elsewhere in the provinces, local populations collaborated with professionals in the production of theatrical frescoes celebrating regional and national history. Parisian turn-of-the-century popular theaters included: Louis Lumet's Théâtre Civique, the Théâtre Populaire de Belleville, and the Théâtre du Peuple at Clichy. In 1902 Firmin Gémier and Romain Rolland produced *Le 14 Juillet*, a spectacular commemoration of the French Revolution, with a cast of one hundred amateur and professional actors. Rolland proclaimed the popular theater ideal: «Que toutes les classes aient place sur la scène, comme sur les gradins du théâtre, mais en qualité d'hommes égaux et fraternels, et non d'ordres rivaux et hiérarchisés» (*Le Théâtre du Peuple*, Paris: Hachette [1913], p. 128).

3. Jean Duvignaud, *Le Théâtre et après* (Paris: Casterman, 1971), p. 18.

4. In the same year, 1927, Artaud and Roger Vitrac opened their Théâtre de la Cruauté in Paris, featuring surrealistic drama, while Brecht collaborated with Erwin Piscator in his first season at the Berlin Piscatorbühne.

5. Antonin Artaud, *Le Théâtre et son double* (Paris: Gallimard [1964]), p. 39.

6. Artaud, p. 60.

7. Bertolt Brecht, *Brecht on Theatre*, trans. and ed. John Willett (New York: Hill and Wang, 1957), p. 190.

8. Jacques Lonchampt, «Huit Jours sur la Montagne de l'Ame de Bob Wilson,» *Le Monde*, 14 Sept. 1972, p. 11.

9. Gérard Gélas, *Le Théâtre du Chêne Noir* (Paris: Stock, 1972), p. 105.

10. Emile Copfermann, *Planchon* (Lausanne: Ed. la Cité, 1969), p. 238.

CHAPTER II

1. Although inspiring a host of sectarian and nationalistic plays meant to instruct and unite the populace, theater legislation during the revolutionary period merely succeeded in assuring the post-revolutionary success of melodrama and vaudeville.

2. Jean Vilar, cited in Emile Copfermann, *Le Théâtre populaire, pourquoi?* (Paris: Maspero, 1969), p. 59.

3. Pierre Gaudibert, *Action culturelle: Intégration et/ou subversion* (Paris: Casterman, 1972), p. 9.

4. André de Baecque, *Les Maisons de la culture* (Paris: Seghers, 1967), p. 21.

5. In 1976, there were fifteen *maisons de la culture*: Amiens, Bobigny, Bourges, Chalon-sur-Saone, Creteil, Firminy, Grenoble, La Rochelle, Le Havre, Nevers, Reims, Rennes, Ajaccio, Chambery, and Nanterre.

6. Jean-Paul Sartre, *Un Théâtre de situations*, ed. Michel Contat and Michel Rybalka (Paris: Gallimard, 1973), p. 84.

7. Daniel Jeannot, «L'Influence de Brecht sur le théâtre français,» *Revue de Belles Lettres*, No. 3 (Nov. 1964), p. 15.

8. In many instances, Bertolt Brecht's theatrical approach parallels that of the absurd playwrights. His techniques, therefore, reinforced such aspects of the absurd as: the elimination of the three-act structure and purely psychological analysis and the reintroduction of burlesque characterization and scenic stylization.

9. Arthur Adamov, *Ici et maintenant* (Paris: Gallimard, 1964), p. 46.

10. Adamov, p. 83.

11. Eugène Ionesco, *Notes et contre-notes* (Paris: Gallimard, 1966), p. 141.

12. Brecht's theater dominated the French stage from 1954 to 1958. In 1959 a rash of publications about him as well as an edition of his complete plays appeared. From 1953 to 1969, 23 of his plays in 79 different stagings for a total of 3,000 performances were given before 2,000,000 spectators. Today, although his plays are still frequently produced, theater professionals feel a great need to reinterpret and give them new life. See «Après Brecht,» *L'Arc*, No. 55 (Winter 1974).

13. Roger Planchon with Bettina Knapp, «Théâtre de la Cité,» *Tulane Drama Review*, 9 (1965), 192-93.

14. Georges Michel with Armand Delcampe, «Le Théâtre politique: Opinion d'un auteur,» *Clés pour le spectacle*, No. 8 (Apr. 1971), p. 12.

15. Armand Gatti, cited in G. Goslan and J.-L. Pays, *Gatti aujourd'hui* (Paris: Ed. du Seuil, 1970), p. 29.

16. Armand Gatti, «La Vie imaginaire de l'éboueur Auguste Geai,» *L'Avant-Scène*, No. 272 (15 Sept. 1962), p. 14.

17. Georges Michel, «Quel public? Quelle participation?» *La Nef*, No. 29 (Jan.-Mar. 1967), p. 69.

18. Aimé Césaire, *La Tragédie du Roi Christophe* (Paris: Présence Africaine, 1963), p. 75.

19. Philippe Decraene, «Entretien avec Aimé Césaire à propos de *La Tragédie du Roi Christophe*,» *Le Monde*, 12 May 1965, p. 16.

20. Among the playwrights of the theater of denunciation of the 1960's are

Kateb Yacine, Michel Vinaver, Gabriel Cousin, Fernando Arrabal, and Jean Genet.

21. Despite all Vilar's efforts, workers never composed more than 3 or 4% of the T.N.P. public.

22. Jack Lang, *L'Etat et le théâtre* (Paris: Bibliothèque de droit public, 1968), p.310.

CHAPTER III

1. Bernard Dort, *Théâtre réel: Essais de critique 1967-1970* (Paris: Ed. du Seuil, 1971), p. 221.

2. Michel Butor, *Tourmente* (Paris: Fata-Morgana, 1968), p. 5.

3. The March 22 Movement, originating from Nanterre University and directed by the student activist Daniel Cohn-Bendit, was a leftist protest group, opposing imperialism, capitalism, and university paternalism.

4. Jacqueline Piatier, «L'Heure des poètes,» *Le Monde*, 1 June 1968, p. 11.

5. The Comité d'Action Révolutionnaire, whose members included French artist Jean-Jacques Lebel, actors Julien Beck and Judith Malina of the Living Theatre, adherents of the March 22 Movement, other theater professionals and students, planned and carried out the occupation of the Odéon theater during the night of May 15-16, 1968.

6. The Comité d'Action Révolutionnaire, cited in Gilles Sandier, *Théâtre et combat* (Paris: Stock, 1970), p. 75.

7. Bertrand Poirot-Delpech, «Que ferez-vous en mai?» *Le Monde* (des loisirs), 5 July 1968, p. 1.

8. Jean-Claude Grumberg, «Demain, une fenêtre sur rue,» *L'Avant-Scène*, No. 405 (15 June 1968), p. 15.

9. René Ehni, «Que ferez-vous en novembre?» *L'Avant-Scène*, No. 412 (15 Oct. 1968), p. 29.

10. Ehni, p. 16.

11. Armand Gatti, *Les Treize Soleils de la rue St.-Blaise* (Paris: Ed. du Seuil, 1968), p. 71.

12. Anne-Marie Duguet, «Le Théâtre universitaire: son efficacité et son action pratique sur les milieux étudiants,» *Cahiers Théâtre Louvain*, No. 10-11 (1970), p. 18.

13. «C.R.S.» is the abbreviation for Compagnie Républicaine de Sécurité, the special French riot police force.

14. The Gymnase, symbolically, was founded and grew to prosperity with bourgeois theater in the nineteenth century.

15. Cited in Sylvain Zegel, *Les Idées de mai* (Paris: Gallimard, 1968), p. 222.

16. «Odéon déclaration of May 17, 1968,» cited in Zegel, p. 220.

17. Nicole Zand, «Le C.R.A.C. contre les trois coups,» *Le Monde*, 11 June 1968, p. 15.

18. «La Déclaration de Villeurbanne,» Philippe Madral, *Le Théâtre hors les murs* (Paris: Ed. du Seuil, 1969), p. 246.

19. «La Déclaration de Villeurbanne.»

20. José Valverde, cited in Ellen Appel, Jorg Aufenanger, Alla Budin, *et al.*, «Mai 1968: Les Théâtres populaires et la politique,» n.p. TS (Paris: Institut d'Etudes théâtrales, 1970), pp. 10-11.

21. J.-P. Ronfard, cited in Appel, *et al.*, p. 139.

22. Nicole Zand, «*La Cuisine* à l'usine,» *Le Monde*, 17 June 1968, p. 19.

23. Théâtre de la Commune d'Aubervilliers, «Le Spondegaulanthrope,» [Aubervilliers], 1968, n.p. TS, n. pag.

24. L'Action Culturelle, «La Promenade de M. Dimanche,» Appel, *et al.*, p.143.

25. Bernard Sobel, cited in Appel, *et al.*, p. 114.

26. L'Action Culturelle, «La Culture,» Appel, *et al.*, p. 149.

27. Bertrand Poirot-Delpech, «Politique partout,» *Le Monde*, 25 Mar. 1971, p. 17.

CHAPTER IV

1. L'Association Théâtrale des Etudiants de Paris (A.T.E.P.) was founded in 1959 and directed by Ariane Mnouchkine until 1961. In 1960, the group sponsored a lecture by Sartre («Théâtre épique et théâtre dramatique») at the Sorbonne which brought it 3,000 francs, enough money to stage Lorca's *Noces de sang*.

2. The present forty members of the Théâtre du Soleil receive a salary of 1,750 francs (about $375.00) a month.

3. Bertrand Poirot-Delpech, «*La Cuisine* d'Arnold Wesker,» *Le Monde*, 9-10 Apr. 1967, p. 22.

4. Personal interview with Sophie Lemasson, assistant director of the Théâtre du Soleil, March 21, 1973.

5. Gilles Sandier, *Théâtre et combat* (Paris: Stock, 1970), pp. 226-27.

6. See Chapter III, «May '68 and the Theater» for a discussion of this experience.

7. Claude Morand, «L'Elaboration d'un travail,» *A.T.A.C. Informations*, Apr. 1972, p. 4.

8. Emile Copfermann, «Entretien avec Ariane Mnouchkine,» *Travail Théâtral*, No. 2 (Jan.-Mar. 1971), p. 12.

9. Ariane Mnouchkine and Jean-Claude Penchenet, «L'Aventure du Théâtre du Soleil,» *Preuves*, No. 7 (1971), p. 123.

10. Colette Godard, «Le Théâtre du Soleil au travail: *1793*, un collectif artisanal,» *Le Monde*, 4 May 1972, p. 19.

11. Emile Copfermann, «Où est la différence: premier entretien avec les comé-

diens,» *Travail Théâtral*, No. 2 (Jan.-Mar. 1971), p. 13.

12. Emile Copfermann, «Entretien avec Ariane Mnouchkine,» *Travail Théâtral*, No. 2 (Jan.-Mar. 1971), p. 44.

13. Ariane Mnouchkine and Jean-Claude Penchenet, «L'Aventure du Théâtre du Soleil,» p. 123.

14. Gilles Sandier, *Théâtre et combat*, p. 82.

15. In the fall of 1970, the Théâtre du Soleil began renting a run-down warehouse in the Cartoucherie de Vincennes, a former armaments factory in a Parisian suburb. The troupe has now completely converted the structure into a working theater.

16. Bertrand Poirot-Delpech, «*1793*, par le Théâtre du Soleil,» *Le Monde*, 20 May 1972, p. 25.

17. The more militant members of the troupe perform agit-prop skits when sollicited by special protest groups. Two of their more successful agit-prop ventures were a winter 1972 vignette on prison abuse, «Qui vole un pain va au prison, qui vole des millions va au Palais Bourbon,» performed for Renault workers and a summer 1975 sketch on the military occupation of pasture lands performed for Larzac peasants.

18. Bertrand Poirot-Delpech, «La Mort heureuse du langage: Michel Lonsdale: Aboyer s'il le faut!» *Le Monde*, 13 Jan. 1972, p. 13.

CHAPTER V

1. André Benedetto, «Manifeste d'avril 1966,» *Soirées, Revue de la Nouvelle Compagnie d'Avignon*, No. 7 (Apr. 1966), pp. 1-8.

2. Personal interview with Jean-Marie Lamblard, member of the Nouvelle Compagnie d'Avignon, July 19, 1973.

3. Occitania: The recently coined name for the community of people speaking *occitan*, or any variation of *langue d'oc* (the ensemble of dialects in the southern regions of France where yes is «oc» rather than «oui»). Without definite boundaries, Occitania includes Béarn, Gascogne, Limousin, Auvergne, Languedoc, Vélay, Vivarais, Southern Dauphiné, Provence, Nice, the Aran Valley in Spain and the Torre-Pellice, Piasco, and Villanove-Fontane valleys in Italy. The Occitanian movement, begun in the late 1950's, similar to that of Brittany, groups together people of a similar heritage who demand cultural recognition. Extremists in the movement insist on economic and political independence from the rest of France. See *Les Temps Modernes*, Nos. 324-326 (Aug.-Sept. 1973) for a detailed analysis of Occitania and its problems.

4. In August 1952, the bodies of three English campers were found in Lurs, Provence, near the French national route 96. After an inconclusive investigation, the police arrested Gaston Dominici, an aged peasant. Despite conflicting evidence and

his repeated proclamations of innocence, Dominici was sentenced to die. He was amnestied in 1960 by De Gaulle. In his play *Pourquoi et comment on fait un assassin de Gaston D*, Benedetto shows how the Parisian special investigator built his case on racial prejudice and psychologically aberrant second guesses which not only condemned Dominici but also, by inference, all the peasants of the region.

5. His 1961-1966 repertoire included plays by Aeschylus, Poe, Chekov, Claudel, Beckett, and Arrabal.

6. Françoise Defosse, «La Nouvelle Compagnie d'Avignon,» *Travail Théâtral*, No. 5 (Oct.-Dec. 1971), p. 7.

7. Françoise Kourilsky, «Avec André Benedetto et les comédiens de la Nouvelle Compagnie d'Avignon,» *Travail Théâtral*, No. 5 (Oct.-Dec. 1971), p. 23.

8. In its theater-in-the-theater structure, variety of scenic techniques and multiple characters, *Napalm* is representative of the kind of play used most often by Benedetto to accuse and disparage his favorite *bêtes noires*. *La Chine entre à L'O.N.U.*, which also censures American involvement in Vietnam, and *Gaston D*, which decries French racism, can be grouped under this category.

9. His other major didactic play, *Emballage*, created in cooperation with the cultural committees of Le Havre, demonstrates the socialist tenet: «Ce qui se cache dans la marchandise, c'est l'homme, c'est-à-dire le travail humain, ce qui se cache dans l'homme c'est la marchandise, c'est-à-dire sa force de travail.» Benedetto's didactic plays and interest in the explanation of capitalism were prompted by May '68 and the resulting Villeurbanne theater declaration.

10. The French army in the spring of 1973 took over extensive farmland in the area of Larzac (part of Occitania) on which it has built training camps for its troops. This action provoked a demonstration of some 10,000 peasants and workers.

11. Fos-sur-Mer is one of the new centers of the metallurgical industry in France. When completed, it will be one of the largest industrial complexes in Europe. In 1969, Fos was only a small fishing village.

12. By its overwhelming ritualistic structure and ambiance, *La Madone des Ordures* is representative of some of Benedetto's most original works. *Zone Rouge, feux interdits*, and *Rosa Lux* are polyphonic masses for dead revolutionary heroes, while *Lola Pelican* is a canonization of a fallen saint and *Chant Funèbre pour un soldat américain* an exorcism of the «imperialist devil.»

13. Emile Copfermann, *La Mise en crise théâtrale* (Paris: Maspero, 1972), p. 227.

14. In 1968, high school teacher Gabrielle Russier was arrested and charged with corrupting the morals of one of her students. The student refused to support the accusation, claiming that he had initiated the love affair. Pressure from the boy's parents, who were also teaching colleagues, caused Mlle Russier to commit suicide in prison. This *fait divers* has become a celebrated cause of political radicals who see in the parents' accusation, rather than concern for their child's morality, vengeance against Mlle Russier's active participation in the high school strikes of May '68. See also *Mourir d'aimer*, a film by André Cayatte, 1971.

15. André Benedetto, «Les Incarcérées,» *Soirées*, No. 33 (Dec.-Jan. 1971), p. 2.

16. It is fitting that Benedetto established his theater on the remains of a medieval cemetery, the ideal location proposed by Genet: «La mort serait à la fois plus proche et plus légère, le théâtre plus grave» (Jean Genet, «L'Etrange Mort d'...,» *Oeuvres complètes*, IV, Paris: Gallimard, 1968, 9-10).

17. Françoise Kourilsky, «Avec André Benedetto et les comédiens de la Nouvelle Compagnie d'Avignon,» p. 20.

18. André Benedetto, «Interview d'André Benedetto,» *Zone Rouge, feux interdits* (Paris: P.J. Oswald, 1969), p. 120.

19. In a personal letter, dated Aug. 17, 1973, he writes, «Poésie et révolution manifestent la vie.»

20. Richard Schechner, «*Marat/Sade* Forum with Peter Brook, Leslie Fiedler, Geraldine Lust, Norma Podhoretz, Ian Richardson and Gordon Rogoff,» *Tulane Drama Review*, 10, No. 4 (Summer 1966), 214-37.

CHAPTER VI

*The author wishes to thank the editorial board of the *Educational Theatre Journal* for permission to include this material (reprinted with revisions from *ETJ*, October 1974).

1. Peter Brook, *The Empty Space* (London: Pelican Books, 1968), p. 76.

2. The four major iron trusts of Lorraine merged in the mid 1960's, forming two companies. Rather than experiment to improve the quality of Lorraine ore or attempt to bring other industries into the region, they have pulled most of their operations out of Lorraine. Since 1963, seventeen iron mines and seven metallurgical factories have been closed; 26,000 men have been laid off and 70,000 persons have moved from Lorraine. Now established primarily at Dunkerque (Mer du Nord) and Fos-sur-Mer (Provence), the two major iron and steel manufacturers import their raw materials from Mali, Ghana, and Madagascar where the quality of the ore is high and the cost of labor low. The economy of Lorraine is therefore currently suffering from a worse recession than that which followed the 1929 stock market crash. See publications by the Comité de Défense du Bassin Ferrifère et Sidérurgique, Lorraine (Briey, France).

3. Théâtre Populaire de Lorraine, «Programme 1963-1964,» [Metz] , 1963, n.p., n. pag.

4. Théâtre Populaire de Lorraine, «Programme 1963-1964.»

5. Whereas the usual private theater charges an admission of 15 francs to 50 francs, depending on the location of the seat, the T.P.L. sets one price, 10 francs for students and 12 francs for adults, for all seats.

6. Théâtre Populaire de Lorraine, «Histoire du T.P.L.,» [Metz] , 1970, n.p., n. pag.

7. Personal interview with Jacques Kraemer, October 31, 1972.

8. «Le retour de T.P.L.,» *Metz, image du mois, magazine de l'agglomération messine*, Jan. 1973, p. 29.

9. Brecht, however, explains the allegorical content in projections at the end of each scene which equate the onstage action with Hitler's activity.

10. Nicole Zand, «Compte rendu de *Splendeur et misère de Minette la bonne Lorraine*,» *Le Monde*, 8-9 Mar. 1970, p. 21.

11. Françoise Claire, «Théâtre, chomage, culture et révolution,» *Tribune Socialiste*, 17 Dec. 1970, p. 18.

12. Liquidation was averted by financial loans from other theater troupes.

13. Colette Godard, «*Les Immigrés* par le Théâtre Populaire de Lorraine,» *Le Monde*, 17 June 1972, p. 21.

14. The 4,000,000 immigrants (primarily North African, Portuguese, Italian, and Spanish) in France comprise 30-40% of the nation's work force. Immigrants hold the majority of construction, sanitation, and assembly-line jobs. However, the average salary of an immigrant is only 800 francs a month. Each year, approximately 30,000 immigrants are injured and 900 killed in on-the-job accidents. See Bernard Granotier, *Les Travailleurs immigrés en France* (Paris: Maspero, 1973).

15. In Kraemer's recent plays, *Le Retour du Graully* (1974) and *Noëlle de Joie* (1975), he is as equally concerned with the nature of theater as with the use of capitalist power. The structures of both works are influenced by stylistic devices found in the *nouveau roman*.

16. Except for *Les Immigrés*, all the T.P.L.'s plays include at least three songs; *La Farce du Graully* has five.

17. The T.P.L.'s «yé yé» music, central to the culture of a popular audience, is the contrary of the discordant tonalities used in Brecht's productions to distance his spectators.

CHAPTER VII

1. Cited in Anne-Marie Duguet, «Le Théâtre universitaire; son efficacité et son action pratique sur les milieux étudiants,» *Cahiers Théâtre Louvain*, No. 10-11 (1970), p. 11.

2. Gilles Sandier, «Trois expériences théâtrales: Copi, *La Journée d'une rêveuse*; Arrabal, *Le Cimetière des voitures*; Rabelais (d'après), *Les Guerres picrocholines*,» *La Quinzaine Littéraire*, 1-15 Feb. 1968, p. 27.

3. See Chapter III, «May '68 and the Theater,» for a detailed discussion of this play.

4. Cited in Anne-Marie Duguet, p. 14.

5. Dominique Norès, «Théâtre universitaire et théâtre politique,» *Tribune Socialiste*, 29 May 1969, p. 18.

6. Bertrand Poirot-Delpech, «La République des honnêtes gens,» *Le Monde*, 18-19 May 1969, p. 17.

7. Sponsored by the Ministry of Cultural Affairs, the Aquarium toured seven South American capital cities and won three awards for the best directed play of the year.

8. Having accepted Jean-Louis Barrault's offer to use his warehouse at the Cartoucherie de Vincennes (Jan. 1973), the troupe set about rebuilding the interior of the structure, constructing a playing area, bathroom facilities, safety exits, offices, and wings. From Mar. to Dec. 1973, the actors and technicians spent a minimum of five hours a day doing manual labor and four improvising and rehearsing.

9. Hélène Cingria, «Création collective,» *Le Journal de Genève*, 31 Oct. 1970, p. 11.

10. Youssef's crime is never explained. In «la république des honnêtes gens» an Arab is guilty of being an Arab.

11. «Théâtre de L'Aquarium,» *Bref*, No. 126 (Feb. 1972), p. 8.

12. In an article on urbanization, «Pour les comités de quartier: Libre noir sur la rénovation» in the *Tribune Socialiste* (17 Feb. 1972, pp. 14-15), Michel Mousel states that since 1954, as a direct result of renovation, the equivalent of the population of Toulouse has been forced to leave Paris proper and move to the dormitory cities on its outskirts. As an example of the graft too often rampant in renovation, he cites a project in the Gobelin area. Promoters promised to reconstruct a railroad station in return for land given to them by the government. This reconstruction was, however, contigent upon their building and selling an apartment development on the newly acquired land. The government obligingly contracted to buy the new apartments for subsidized housing, thereby paying not only for the apartments but also for the land it had given away, assuring the promoters a maximum profit, and costing the taxpayers twice as much as if it had directly built the low-cost housing.

13. Mathieu Galey in *Les Nouvelles Littéraires* (13-19 Mar. 1972, p. 25) sarcastically suggests that a performance of *Marchands de Ville* should inaugurate the Montparnasse Tower: «Dommage qu'il n'y ait pas de salle prévue dans la Tour Montparnasse. *Marchands de Ville* aurait été un bon spectacle d'inauguration. A moins qu'on ne le reprenne quand on ouvrira le Centre Culturel du plateau Beaubourg. S'il reste encore quelques survivants du quartier des Halles, ils s'y retrouveront en pays connu.»

14. Jean-Jacques Gautier, «Marchands de Ville,» *Le Figaro*, 26-27 Feb. 1972, p. 28.

15. Théâtre de l'Aquarium, program notes of *Gob, ou le journal d'un homme normal*, [Paris], 1973, n.p., n. pag.

16. Théâtre de l'Aquarium, program notes of *Gob*.

17. In September 1974, Leroy and Mme Mayeur (now Mme Leroy) were released from custody. Jean-Pierre Flahaut was released in July 1975. To date (summer 1976) the murder remains unsolved.

18. Jean-Louis Clavet, «Le Notaire, sa fiancée, le juge . . . et les journaux,» *Politique Hebdo*, 18 May 1972, p. 7.

19. See the Philippe Gavi article «Bruay-en-Artois: seul un bourgeois aurait pu faire çà.» *Les Temps Modernes*, No. 312-313 (July-Aug. 1972), pp. 155-260, for an analysis of how different newspapers treated the affair.

20. Robert Carm and Serge Bernard, «Quoi qu'il advienne je ferai front, dit Monique Mayeur, la fiancée du notaire,» *France-Soir*, 10 May 1972, p. 3.

21. Victor Franco, «Le Juge Pascal marche sur une poudrière,» *Le Journal du dimanche*, 7 May 1972, p. 4.

22. «Et maintenant ils massacrent nos enfants: Il n'y a qu'un bourgeois pour avoir fait ça.» *La Cause du peuple*, No. 23 (May 1972), p. 2.

23. Anne Fohr, «Une âme de papier, *Gob*, par le Théâtre de l'Aquarium,»

Le Nouvel Observateur, 24-31 Dec. 1973, p. 9.

24. If the original project had been completely followed, the ambiguity of the Aquarium's political position would have been eliminated by the role of the Prompter. His political observations would have served as critical counterpoint to the items on Bruay-en-Artois. However, as the troupe approached the opening deadline without having been able to integrate successfully the Prompter into the rest of the play, it was forced to drop the role.

CHAPTER VIII

1. Bertrand Poirot-Delpech, «Relâche chez les héritiers de Vilar,» *Le Monde*, 13 July 1972, p. 15.

2. Poirot-Delpech, p. 15.

3. In 1956, Jack Lang founded the experimental and highly politicized international theater festival at Nancy. The festival is held every other year in the spring.

4. Emile Copfermann, «Le Système du subventionnement,» *Travail Théâtral*, No. 12 (July-Sept. 1973), p. 18.

5. Renée Saurel, «Deniers publics ou cassette royale, I?» *Les Temps Modernes*, No. 320 (Mar. 1973), p. 1720.

6. Roger Blin, «Deux metteurs en scène répondent à M. Saint-Marc,» *Le Monde*, 2-3 Nov. 1969, p. 17.

7. Maurice Druon, «M. Maurice Druon refusera de subventionner les entreprises culturelles jugées subversives,» *Le Monde*, 4 May 1973, p. 26.

8. Jean-Louis Barrault, «Le Clairon de la répression culturelle,» *Le Monde*, 11 May 1973, p. 1.

9. Marcel Achard, «L'Académie Française reçoit M. Jean-Jacques Gautier,» *Le Monde*, 18 May 1973, p. 24.

10. Maurice Druon, «M. Maurice Druon expose ses conceptions sur la préservation du patrimoine artistique et l'aide à la création,» *Le Monde*, 25 May 1973, pp. 6-7.

11. The subsidies awarded by the Secretary of State for Cultural Affairs in 1974-1975 to the troupes studied in this work were as follows: Théâtre du Soleil, 1,000,000 FF; Théâtre Populaire de Lorraine, 450,000 FF; The Aquarium, 30,000 FF; André Benedetto, 80,000 FF.

12. Renée Saurel, «Deniers publics ou cassette royale, II?» *Les Temps Modernes*, No. 321 (Apr. 1973), p. 1908.

13. Georges Michel, «La Cour des Miracles,» n.d., n.p. TS, n. pag.

14. Darko Suvin, «Organizational Meditation: The Paris Commune Theater Law,» *Tulane Drama Review*, 13, No. 4 (Summer 1969), 30.

15. Jack Lang, *L'Etat et le théâtre* (Paris: Bibliothèque de droit public, 1968), p. 257.

16. In addition to the groups founded after May '68 which practice collective creation, notably l'Acte, le Groupe Kiss, le TEX, l'Orbe, and l'Arche de Noë, more and more theatrical neophytes adhere to group creativity. Of the fourteen troupes participating in the First National Festival of University Theater in May 1974, ten presented collective creations. Recently (1975-1976) several young writers from the East of France—Jean-Paul Wenzel, Michel Deutch, Robert Gironès—have begun to practice a collective dramaturgy. The author subjects his text, often based on every-day reality, to a group of actors who criticize and modify it according to a joint conception of the *mise en scène.*

17. Emile Copfermann, «Le Système du subventionnement,» p. 37.

BIBLIOGRAPHY

Background and History

Achard, Marcel. «L'Académie Française reçoit M. Jean-Jacques Gautier.» *Le Monde*, 18 May 1973, pp. 23-24.

Adamov, Arthur. *Ici et Maintenant*. Paris: Gallimard, 1964.

«Après Brecht.» (Ed. Robert Abirached) *L'Arc*, No. 55 (Winter 1974).

Bablet, Denis. «Entretien avec Armand Gatti.» *Travail Théâtral*, No. 3 (Apr.-June 1971), pp. 3-21.

———. *Les Révolutions scéniques au XXe siècle*. Paris: Editions XXe siècle, 1976.

Baby, Yvonne. «Le Territoire de Roger Planchon.» *Le Monde*, 2 May 1974, pp. 19-20.

Baecque, André de. *Les Maisons de la culture*. Paris: Seghers, 1967.

Barba, Eugenio. «Theater and Revolution.» *International Theater Information*, Summer 1970, pp. 7-9.

Barrault, Jean-Louis. «Le Clairon de la répression culturelle.» *Le Monde*, 11 May 1973, pp. 1, 17.

Baxandall, Lee. «The Revolutionary Moment.» *Tulane Drama Review*, 13, No. 2 (Winter 1978), 92-107.

Beigbeder, Marc. *Le Théâtre en France depuis la libération*. Paris: Bordas, 1959.

Bermel, Albert. «Jean Vilar: Unadorned Theater for the Greatest Number.» *Tulane Drama Review*, 5, No. 2 (Winter 1960), 24-43.

Blin, Roger and Chéreau, Patrice. «Deux metteurs-en-scène répondent à M. Saint-Marc.» *Le Monde*, 2 Nov. 1969, p. 17.

Bonnerot, Sylviane. *Visages du théâtre contemporain*. Paris: Masson et Cie., 1971.

Bureau de l'A.J.T. «Le Jeune Théâtre dans la crise.» *Travail Théâtral*, No. 15 (Apr.-June 1974), pp. 132-40.

Césaire, Aimé. *La Tragédie du Roi Christophe*. Paris: Présence Africaine, 1963.

Copeau, Jacques. «Le Théâtre populaire: un document.» *Théâtre Populaire*, No. 36 (Winter 1959), pp. 77-114.

Copfermann, Emile. *La Mise en crise théâtrale*. Paris: Maspero, 1972.

———. *Planchon*. Lausanne: Ed. la Cité, 1969.

———. «La Résistible Découverte du théâtre de M.B. Brecht en France.» *Les Lettres Françaises*, No. 1276 (26 Mar.-2 Apr. 1969), pp. 14-15.

———. «Le Système du subventionnement.» *Travail Théâtral*, No. 12 (July-Sept. 1973), pp. 13-39.

———. *Le Théâtre populaire, pourquoi?* Paris: Maspero, 1969.

Corvin, Michel. *Le Théâtre nouveau en France*. Paris: Presses Universitaires Françaises, 1974.

Dandrel, Louis. «Armand Gatti: Dans le maquis de la contre-culture.» *Le Monde*, 29 June 1973, p. 14.

———. «Mai 68, il y a cinq ans: Ce qu'a pu signifier le mot culture.» *Le Monde*, 25 May 1973, p. 21.

Decraene, Philippe. «Entretien avec Aimé Césaire à propos de *La Tragédie du Roi Christophe*.» *Le Monde*, 12 May 1965, p. 16.

Dejean, Jean-Luc. *Le Théâtre français aujourd'hui*. Paris: Alliance Française-F. Nathan, 1971.

Demarcy, Richard. *Eléments d'une sociologie du spectacle*. Paris: Union Générale d'éditions, Collection 10/18, 1973.

Dort, Bernard. *Théâtre public: Essais de critique 1953-1966*. Paris: Ed. du Seuil, 1967.

———. *Théâtre réel: Essais de critique 1967-1970*. Paris: Ed. du Seuil, 1971.

Druon, Maurice. «Le Débat à l'Assemblée Nationale sur la liberté d'expression: M. Maurice Druon expose ses conceptions sur la préservation du patrimoine artistique et l'aide à la création.» *Le Monde*, 25 May 1973, pp. 6-7.

———. «M. Maurice Druon refusera de subventionner les entreprises culturelles jugées subversives.» *Le Monde*, 4 May 1973, pp. 1, 26.

Dutourd, Jean. *Le Paradoxe du critique suivi de Sept Saisons: Impressions de théâtre*. Paris: Flammarion, 1972.

Duvignaud, Jean and Lagoutte, Jean. *Le Théâtre contemporain: Culture et contre-culture*. Paris: Larousse, 1974.

Esprit, No. 338 [special issue on theater], (May 1965).

Even, Martin. «De Nancy à Chaillot: L'Aventure théâtrale de Jack Lang.» *Le Monde*, 8 June 1973, p. 19.

Galey, Mathieu. «Le Théâtre populaire à la croisée des chemins.» *La Nouvelle Revue Française*, No. 245 (May 1973), pp. 106-09.

Gatti, Armand. «La Vie imaginaire de l'éboueur Auguste Geai.» *L'Avant-Scène*, No. 272 (15 Sept. 1962).

Gautier, Jean-Jacques. *Théâtre aujourd'hui. Dix ans de critique dramatique et des entretiens avec M. Abadi sur le théâtre et la critique.* Paris: Julliard, 1972.

Gélas, Gérard. *Le Théâtre du Chêne Noir.* Paris: Stock, 1972.

Gisselbrecht, André. «Avignon après Vilar.» *La Nouvelle Critique.* No. 54 (June 1972), pp. 63-69.

Godard, Colette. «La mise en sommeil de Chaillot et d'autres compagnies marque un recul dans la politique théâtrale de M. Guy.» *Le Monde*, 8 July 1976, p. 15.

Gontard, Denis. *La Décentralisation théâtrale en France (1895-1952).* Paris: Sedès, 1974.

Gozlan, Gérard and Pays, Jean-Louis. *Gatti, aujourd'hui.* Paris: Ed. du Seuil, 1970.

Ionesco, Eugène. *Notes et contre-notes.* Paris: Gallimard, 1966.

–––. «Le Théâtre ne peut évoluer sans être dépolitisé.» *Le Figaro Littéraire*, 29 June 1972, pp. 13, 18.

Jacquart, Emmanuel. *Le Théâtre de dérision.* Paris: Gallimard, 1974.

Jeannet, Daniel. «L'Influence de Brecht sur le théâtre français.» *Revue de Belles-Lettres*, No. 3 (Nov. 1964), pp. 15-20.

Jeanson, Francis. *L'Action Culturelle dans la cité.* Paris: Ed. du Seuil, 1973.

Kern, Edith. «Brecht's Epic Theatre and the French Stage.» *Symposium*, No. 16 (Spring 1962), pp. 28-35.

Kilker, James and Marie. «The Druon Affair: A Documentary.» *Educational Theater Journal*, 26, No. 3 (Oct. 1974), 365-76.

Knapp, Bettina. *Offstage Voices: Interviews with Modern French Dramatists.* New York: Whitson Publishing Co., 1976.

Kourilsky, Françoise and Champagne, Lenora. «Political Theater in France since 1968.» *Drama Review*, 19, No. 2 (Summer 1975), 44-52.

Kourilsky, Françoise. «Politics and Subsidy in France.» *Performance*, 2, No. 1 (1973), pp. 9-10.

Lang, Jack. *L'Etat et le théâtre.* Paris: Bibliothèque de droit public, 1968.

Laurent, Jeanne. *La République des Beaux-Arts.* Paris: Julliard, 1965.

Laville, Pierre. «Aimé Césaire et Jean-Marie Serreau: Un acte politique et poétique; *La Tragédie du Roi Christophe, Une Saison au Congo.*» Paris: *Voies de la création théâtrale,* II. Ed. C.N.R.S., 1970, 237-96.

Leclerc, Guy. *Le T.N.P. de Jean Vilar.* Paris: Union Générale d'éditions, Collection 10/18, 1971.

Lee, Vera. *Quest for a Public French Popular Theatre since 1945*. Cambridge, Mass.: Schenkman Publishing Co., 1971.

Leirens, Jean. «Approches du théâtre contemporain: Théâtre engagé, qu'est-ce que cela veut dire?» *Clés pour le Spectacle*, No. 8 (Apr. 1971), pp. 9-10.

Lonchampt, Jacques. «Huit Jours sur la Montagne de l'Ame de Bob Wilson.» *Le Monde*, 14 Sept. 1972, p. 11.

Madral, Philippe. *Le Théâtre hors les murs*. Paris: Ed. du Seuil, 1969.

Michel, Georges. *La Promenade du dimanche*. Paris: Gallimard, 1967.

———. «Quel public? Quelle participation?» *La Nef*, No. 29 (Jan.-Mar. 1967), pp. 64-70.

Michel, Georges with Delcampe, Armand. «Le Théâtre politique: Opinion d'un auteur.» *Clés pour le Spectacle*, No. 8 (Apr. 1971), pp. 12-15.

O'Connor, Garry. *French Theatre Today*. Bath, England: The Pitman Press, 1975.

Olivier, Claude. «La Réorganisation du T.N.P.: Oui!» *Les Lettres Françaises*, 9 Apr. 1972, p. 11.

Orenstein, Gloria. *The Theater of the Marvelous*. New York: New York University Press, 1975.

Partisans. Ed. Emile Copfermann and Georges Dupré. No. 36, «Théâtres et politique» (Feb.-Mar. 1967); No. 47, «Théâtres et politique, bis» (Apr.-May 1969).

Planchon, Roger with Knapp, Bettina. «Théâtre de la Cité.» *Tulane Drama Review*, 9, No. 3 (April 1965), 190-93.

Planchon, Roger et al. «Un Théâtre qui mobilise.» *Preuves*, No. 18 (Summer 1974), pp. 47-60.

Poirot-Delpech, Bertrand. *Au soir le soir 1960-1970*. Paris: Mercure de France, 1969.

———. «Politique partout.» *Le Monde*, 25 Mar. 1971, pp. 17-20.

———. «Relâche chez les héritiers de Vilar.» *Le Monde*, 13 July 1972, p. 15.

———. «Le Théâtre en 1970, un art désuni: En avoir pour son argent.» *Le Monde*, 22 July 1970, pp. 1, 14; «Le Théâtre public en 1970: Entre deux défiances.» 23 July 1970, p. 11; «Le Théâtre en marge de 1970: Guerilla ou gymnastique.» 24 July 1970, p. 12.

———. «Une Année de théâtre: Pauvre France.» *Le Monde*, 24 July 1971, pp. 1, 15; «Héritier ou pas.» 25-26 July 1971, p. 10; «Mnouchkine ou Bob Wilson?» 27 July 1971, p. 14.

Poulet, Jacques. «Introduction au théâtre populaire.» *La Nouvelle Critique*. No. 65 (June-July 1973), pp. 25-34.

———. «Un Théâtre en procès.» *La Nouvelle Critique*. No. 54 (June 1972), pp. 71-77.

Ristat, Jean. «Ecriture, théâtre, politique: entretien avec Jean Thibaudet.» *Les Lettres Françaises*, 7 June 1972, pp. 3-5.

Sandier, Gilles. *Théâtre et combat*. Paris: Stock, 1970.

Sarrazac, Jean-Pierre. «L'Ecriture au présent.» *Travail Théâtral*, No. 18-19 (Jan.-June 1975), pp. 55-80.

Sarrazin, Maurice. *Comédien dans une troupe*. Toulouse: Grenier de Toulouse, 1970.

Sartre, Jean-Paul. *Un Théâtre de situations*. Ed. Michel Contat and Michel Rybalka. Paris: Gallimard, 1973.

Saurel, Renée. «Chéreau et Planchon, excommuniés.» *Les Temps Modernes*, No. 284 (Mar. 1970), pp. 1538-45.

———. «Deniers publics ou cassette royale? I.» *Les Temps Modernes*, No. 320 (Mar. 1973), pp. 1710-21; II, No. 321 (Apr. 1973), pp. 1907-18.

———. «Le Monstre froid et le théâtre, I.» *Les Temps Modernes*, No. 283 (Feb. 1970), pp. 1294-1303; II, No. 286 (May 1970), pp. 1897-1906; III, No. 289 (Aug.-Sept. 1970), pp. 556-63.

Simon, Alfred. «Théâtre et désastre. Qui croit encore au théâtre populaire?» *Esprit*, No. 393 (June 1970), pp. 1136-56.

Taquet, Yvonne. «Le Théâtre en marge.» *Cahiers Littéraires de l'O.R.T.F.*, No. 9 (31 Jan.-13 Feb. 1971), pp. 35-36.

Temkine, Raymonde. *L'Entreprise théâtre*. Paris: Cujas, 1967.

———. «Feu le T.N.P. de Chaillot.» *Europe*, No. 523-24 (Nov.-Dec. 1972), pp. 279-84.

Le Théâtre 1968–I: Le Baroque. Ed. Fernando Arrabal. Paris: Christian Bourgois, 1968.

Le Théâtre 1969–I: Mai 68. Ed. Fernando Arrabal. Paris: Christian Bourgois, 1969.

Le Théâtre 1970–I: Le Théâtre marginal. Ed. Fernando Arrabal. Paris: Christian Bourgois, 1970.

Vessillier, Michèle. *La Crise du théâtre privé*. Paris: Presses Universitaires de France, 1974.

Vilar, Jean. «L'Art du théâtre n'est pas né un jour.» *Travail Théâtral*, No. 5 (Oct.-Dec. 1971), pp. 110-11.

———. *De la tradition théâtrale*. Paris: Gallimard, 1963.

———. *Le Théâtre service public et autres textes*. Paris: Gallimard, 1975.

Willener, Alfred. *L'Image-Action de la société ou la politisation culturelle*. Paris: Ed. du Seuil, 1970.

May '68 and the Theater

Adrien, Philippe. *La Baye*. Paris: Ed. du Seuil, 1968.

Appel, Ellen, *et al.* «Mai 1968: Les théâtres populaires et la politique.» n.p. TS., Paris: Institut d'Etudes Théâtrales, 1970.

Aron, Raymond. *La Révolution introuvable*. Paris: Fayard, 1968.

Arrabal, Fernando. «The Groupuscule of My Heart.» Trans. Bettina Knapp. *Tulane Drama Review*, 13, No. 4 (Summer 1969), 123-38.

———. Théâtre VII: Théâtre de guerilla: Et ils passèrent des menottes aux fleurs: L'Aurore rouge et noire. Paris: Christian Bourgois, 1969.

Ayache, Alain. *Les Citations de la révolution de mai*. Paris: J.-J. Pauvert, 1968.

«Jean-Louis Barrault déplore de n'avoir reçu aucune directive.» *Le Monde*, 25 May 1968, p. 10.

Bensaid, Daniel and Weber, Henri. *Mai, 1968: Une répétition générale*. Paris: Maspero, 1968.

Besançon, Julien. *Les Murs ont la parole*. Paris: Tchon, 1968.

Butor, Michel. *Tourmente*. Paris: Fata-Morgana, 1968.

Campos, Christophe. «Experiments for the People of Paris.» *Theatre Quarterly*, 2 (Oct.-Dec. 1972), 52-67.

Certeau, Michel de. *La Prise de la parole*. Paris: Desclée de Brouwer, 1968.

Charrière, Christian. *Les Printemps des enragés*. Paris: Fayard, 1968.

«150 Comédiens se désolidarisent de la direction de leur centrale.» *Le Monde*, 25 May 1968, p. 6.

Copfermann, Emile. «La Rentrée théâtrale: Entre le conformisme et la contestation.» *Les Lettres Françaises*, 4-19 Sept. 1968, p. 22.

Dansette, Adrien. *Mai 1968*. Paris: Plon, 1971.

Demarcy, Richard. «Mai 1968, un mois de grève active au Théâtre de la Commune.» n.p. TS., Aubervilliers: Théâtre de la Commune d'Aubervilliers, June 1968.

Dimitriadis, Dimitri. «Le Prix de la révolte au marché noir.» Trans. Richard Kalisz. *Théâtre et Université*, No. 11 (Sept.-Oct. 1967).

Durandeaux, Jacques. *Les Journées de mai 1968*. Paris: Desclée de Brouwer, 1968.

Ehni, René. «Que ferez-vous en novembre?» *L'Avant-Scène*, No. 412 (15 Oct. 1968).

Gatti, Armand. *Les Treize Soleils de la rue St.-Blaise*. Paris: Ed. du Seuil, 1968.

Gaudibert, Pierre. *Action culturelle: Intégration et/ou subversion*. Paris: Casterman, 1972.

Goustine, Luc de. *10 mai 1968*. Paris: Ed. du Seuil, 1968.

Grumberg, Jean-Claude. «Demain, une fenêtre sur rue.» *L'Avant-Scène*, No. 405 (15 June 1968).

Hampton, Charles C. «Polarity and Stasis: Drama as Reflection of a Revolution.» *Yale Theatre*, 2, No. 3 (Winter 1969), 39-42.

Lebel, Jean-Jacques. «Notes on Political Street Theatre, Paris: 1968-1969.» *Tulane Drama Review*, 13, No. 4 (Summer 1969), 111-18.

———. *Procès du festival d'Avignon: Supermarché de la culture.* Paris: Belfond, 1968.

Maulnier, Thierry. «Après la grande secousse.» *La Revue de Paris*, No. 11 (Nov. 1969), pp. 133-35.

Michel, Jacques. «Les Artistes dans la mêlée, le happening permanent.» *Le Monde*, 25 May 1968, p. 10.

Morin, Edgar, *et al. Mai 1968: la brèche, premières réflexions sur les événements.* Paris: Fayard, 1968.

Mouvement du 22 mars. *Ce n'est qu'un début, continuons le combat.* Paris: Maspero, 1968.

Norès, Dominique. «Le Défi de mai et la révolution au théâtre.» *Les Lettres Nouvelles*, Sept.-Oct. 1968, pp. 162-68.

Piatier, Jacqueline. «L'Heure des poètes.» *Le Monde*, 1 June 1968, p. 11.

Poèmes de la révolution de mai. Paris: Ed. Caractères, 1968.

Poirot-Delpech, Bertrand. «Que ferez-vous en mai?» *Le Monde* (des loisirs), 5 July 1968, p. 1.

Rioux, Lucien and Backmann, René. *11 mai 1968: L'Explosion de mai.* Paris: Laffont, 1968.

Sandier, Gilles. «Théâtre d'après mai.» *La Quinzaine Littéraire*, No. 60 (1-15 Nov. 1968), p. 28.

Seale, Patrick and McConville, Maureen. *Drapeaux rouges sur la France.* Paris: Mercure de France, 1968.

Servan-Schreiber, J.-J. *Le Réveil de la France.* Paris: Denoël, 1968.

Simon, Alfred. «The Theatre in May.» *Yale French Studies*, No. 46 (1971), pp. 139-48.

Théâtre de la Commune d'Aubervilliers. «Mai 1968: Le Spondégaulantrope, Du Tracassin à la chie-en-lit.» n.p. TS., Aubervilliers: Théâtre de la Commune d'Aubervilliers, 1968.

Théâtre de l'Epée de Bois. «Three Street Plays: Paris 1968; *Dis May, Repression, At the Polls: Electoral Opera-Bouffe.*» *Tulane Drama Review*, 13, No. 3 (Summer 1969), 119-22.

Théâtre universitaire de Nancy. «On the Difficulty of Putting Politics in Charge.» *Yale Theatre*, 2, No. 3 (Winter 1969), 43-50.

Thénevin, Jean. *Octobre à Angoulême.* Paris: Gallimard, 1970.

Thibaud, Paul. «Imaginons . . . » *Esprit*, 372 (June-July 1968), 1031-36.

Thibaudeau, Jean. *Mai 1968 en France*. Paris: Ed. du Seuil, 1970.

Touraine, Alain. *Le Mouvement de mai ou le communisme utopique*. Paris: Ed. du Seuil, 1968.

Wesker, Arnold. *La Cuisine*. Trans. Philippe Léotard. Paris: Gallimard, 1967.

Zand, Nicole. «Le C.R.A.C. contre les trois coups. *Le Monde*, 10 June 1968, p. 15.

———. «La Cuisine à l'usine.» *Le Monde*, 16-17 June 1968, p. 19.

———. «Ex-Odéon Forum.» *Le Monde*, 16 May 1968, p. 4.

Zegel, Sylvain. *Les Idées de mai*. Paris: Gallimard, 1968.

Théâtre du Soleil

Bablet, Denis. «Rencontres avec le Théâtre du Soleil.» *Travail Théâtral*, No. 18-19 (Jan.-June 1975), pp. 5-39.

———. «Une Scénographie pour *1793*.» *Travail Théâtral*, No. 9 (Oct.-Dec. 1972), pp. 97-107.

Bartoli, François. «Quelques formes de participation théâtrale.» n.p. TS., Paris: Institut d'Etudes Théâtrales, 1969.

Cartier, Jacqueline. «Ariane Mnouchkine met la Révolution dans une poudrière.» *France-Soir*, 2 Nov. 1970, p. 17.

«Le Combat d'Ariane Mnouchkine.» *Le Nouvel Observateur*, 2-8 Apr. 1973, p. 44.

Copfermann, Emile. «Second Entretien avec les comédiens.» *Travail Théâtral*, No. 8 (July-Sept. 1972), pp. 28-33.

———. «*1793*, Une histoire mise à jour.» *Travail Théâtral*, No. 8 (July-Sept. 1972), pp. 51-56.

———. «Entretien avec Ariane Mnouchkine.» *Travail Théâtral*, No. 2 (Jan.-Mar. 1971), pp. 3-12.

———. «Milan ouvert au Théâtre du Soleil.» *Les Lettres Françaises*, 25 Nov. 1970, pp. 13-14.

———. «Où est la différence: Premier entretien avec les comédiens.» *Travail Théâtral*, No. 2 (Jan.-Mar. 1971), pp. 13-18.

———. «Le Théâtre du Soleil: *L'Arbre sorcier, Jérôme et la tortue*.» *Les Lettres Françaises*, 11 Apr. 1968, pp. 21-22.

Davis, Yvon *et al.* «Première ébauche, entretien avec Ariane Mnouchkine.» *Théâtre/Public: Revue Bi-mestrielle de l'Ensemble Théâtral de Gennevilliers*, Summer 1975, pp. 4-6.

Domenach, Nicolas. «Splendeurs et décadences d'une création collective.» *Esprit*, No. 447 (June 1975), pp. 965-82.

Dort, Bernard. «Entre le passé et le futur: *L'Age d'or* au Théâtre du Soleil.» *Travail Théâtral*, No. 20 (July-Oct. 1975), pp. 78-84.

———. «L'Illusion politique.» *Politique Hebdo*, 12 Jan. 1971, p. 39.

Dumur, Guy. «Songes des nuits d'hiver.» *Le Nouvel Observateur*, 28 Feb.-6 Mar. 1968, p. 39.

Ezine, Jean-Louis. «Entretien avec Ariane Mnouchkine.» *Les Nouvelles Littéraires*, 3 Mar. 1975, p. 3.

François, Guy Claude. «A chaque spectacle sa scénographie.» *Travail Théâtral*, No. 2 (Jan.-Mar. 1971), pp. 19-21.

Galey, Mathieu. «L'Age d'or première ébauche.» *Le Quotidien de Paris*, 10 Mar. 1975, p. 8.

Godard, Colette. «*L'Age d'or* par le Théâtre du Soleil: Quatre vallées pour l'an 2000.» *Le Monde*, 12 Mar. 1975, pp. 1, 13.

———. «Le Théâtre: *1789*, une création française à Milan par la compagnie du Théâtre du Soleil.» *Le Monde*, 17 Nov. 1970.

———. «Le Théâtre du Soleil au travail: *1793*, un collectif artisanal.» *Le Monde*, 4 May 1972, p. 19.

Gousselard, Jack. «Arlequin 75.» *Le Point*, No. 130 (17 Mar. 1975), pp. 120-21.

Kirby, Victoria N. «Reports on *1789*.» *Tulane Drama Review*, 15, No. 4 (Fall 1971), 73-91.

Kirkland, Christopher D. «Théâtre du Soleil's *The Golden Age, First Draft*.» *Drama Review*, 19, No. 2 (Summer 1975), 53-60.

Kourilsky, Françoise. «Les Acteurs hors théâtre,» pp. 44-50; «De *1789* à *1793*: Entretien avec Ariane Mnouchkine,» pp. 22-25; «L'Entreprise,» pp. 19-20; «Entretien avec les comédiens,» pp. 32-38; «Notes sur l'élaboration du spectacle,» pp. 26-31, *Travail Théâtral*, No. 8 (July-Sept. 1972).

Lazzari, Arturo. «*1789*, La Révolution française vue du peuple.» *Travail Théâtral*, No. 2 (Jan.-Mar. 1971), pp. 34-37.

Marc'O. «Création collective.» *La Nef*, No. 29 (Jan.-Mar. 1969), pp. 74-80.

Mnouchkine, Ariane and Penchenet, Jean-Claude. «L'Aventure du Théâtre du Soleil.» *Preuves*, No. 7 (Fall 1971), pp. 119-27.

Mnouchkine, Ariane *et al.* «Ariane, c'est une grande chose qui commence: Table ronde sur le Théâtre du Soleil.» *Esprit*, No. 447 (June 1975), pp. 945-46.

Morand, Claude. «L'Elaboration d'un travail.» *A.T.A.C. Informations*, Apr. 1972, pp. 2-5.

Moscoso, Roberto. «Un Théâtre pour chaque spectacle.» *Travail Théâtral*, No. 2 (Jan.-Mar. 1971), pp. 22-27.

Mounier, Catherine. «Les Règles du jeu.» *Travail Théâtral*, No. 18-19 (Jan.-June 1975), pp. 40-54.

———. «Rôles et personnages.» *Travail Théâtral*, No. 8 (July-Sept. 1972), pp. 39-46.

Nourissier, François. «*L'Age d'or*: Militantisme et perfection technique.» *Le Figaro*, 12 Mar. 1975, p. 28.

Poirot-Delpech, Bertrand. «Art dramatique et lutte des classes.» *Le Monde* (des loisirs), 8 Nov. 1968, p. 1.

———. «*La Cuisine* d'Arnold Wesker.» *Le Monde*, 9-10 Apr. 1967, p. 22.

———. «*1793* par le Théâtre du Soleil.» *Le Monde*, 20 May 1972, p. 25.

———. «L'Evénement de la saison: *1789* par le Théâtre du Soleil.» *Le Monde*, 14 Jan. 1971, p. 3.

———. «La Mort heureuse du langage; Michel Lonsdale: Aboyer s'il le faut!» *Le Monde*, 13 Jan. 1972, p. 13.

Raskine, Michel, *et al.* «*1789* par le Théâtre du Soleil.» n.p. TS., Paris: Institut d'Etudes Théâtrales, 1971.

Roy, Claude. «Shakespeare chez les lions.» *Le Nouvel Observateur*, 6-13 Mar. 1968, p. 44.

Sandier, Gilles. «La Dynamique révolutionnaire.» *La Quinzaine Littéraire*, 16 June 1972, p. 25.

Simon, Alfred. «Un Rêve vécu du théâtre populaire.» *Esprit*, No. 447 (June 1975), pp. 933-44.

Théâtre du Soleil. *L'Age d'or: Première ébauche*. Paris: Stock, 1975.

———. *1789, La Révolution doit s'arrêter à la perfection du bonheur*. Paris: Stock, 1971.

———. *1793, La Cité révolutionnaire est de ce monde*. Paris: Stock, 1972.

«Le Théâtre du Soleil est menacé de disparaître.» *Le Monde*, 29 Mar. 1973, p. 38.

Varenne, Françoise. «Théâtre du Soleil: la Commedia dell' arte 1975.» *Le Figaro*, 6 Mar. 1975, p. 32.

Zand, Nicole. «Au Cirque de Montmartre: Le Théâtre du Soleil crée *La Cuisine* de Wesker.» *Le Monde*, 9 Apr. 1967, p. 17.

André Benedetto

Benedetto, André. *Aie! Les Lunes de Fos: Chronique d'un enlisement*. Paris: P.J. Oswald, 1975.

———. *Alexandra K*. Paris: P.J. Oswald, 1975.

———. *Auguste et Peter suivi de Lola Pélican*. Paris: P.J. Oswald, 1971.

———. *Chant Funèbre pour un soldat américain*. Paris: P.J. Oswald, 1972.

———. *La Chine entre à L'O.N.U.* Paris: P.J. Oswald, 1971.

———. «Des héritiers de l'inter-dit.» *La Nouvelle Critique*, No. 88 (Nov. 1975), pp. 32-33.

———. *Emballage.* Paris: P.J. Oswald, 1970.

———. *Esclamonda.* Paris: P.J. Oswald, 1975.

———. «Les Incarcérées.» *Soirées, Revue de la Nouvelle Compagnie d'Avignon*, No. 33 (Dec.-Jan. 1971).

———. *La Madone des Ordures.* Paris: P.J. Oswald, 1973.

———. «Manifeste d'avril 1966.» *Soirées, Revue de la Nouvelle Compagnie d'Avignon*, No. 7 (Apr. 1966), pp. 1-8.

———. *Napalm.* Paris: P.J. Oswald, 1968.

———. «Ordinateur pour Safari.» *Soirées, Revue de la Nouvelle Compagnie d'Avignon*, No. 55 (Mar.-Apr. 1975).

———. «Le Petit Héros populaire et son public.» *Travail Théâtral*, No. 21 (Oct.-Dec. 1975), pp. 40-47.

———. *Le Petit Train de M. Kamodé.* Paris: P.J. Oswald, 1969.

———. *Pourquoi et comment on fait un assassin de Gaston D.* Paris: P.J. Oswald, 1975.

———. *Rosa Lux.* Paris: P.J. Oswald, 1970.

———. *Urgent Crieur.* Paris: P.J. Oswald, 1965.

———. *Zone Rouge, feux interdits.* Paris: P.J. Oswald, 1969.

Cingria, Hélène. «XXIIIe Festival d'Avignon: Théâtre parallèle.» *Les Lettres Françaises*, 27 Aug.-3 Sept. 1969, p. 18.

Dandrel, Louis. «Théâtre et musique à Avignon: André Benedetto au Cloître des Carmes.» *Le Monde*, 19 July 1973, p. 23.

Defosse, Françoise. «La Nouvelle Compagnie d'Avignon.» *Travail Théâtral*, No. 5 (Oct.-Dec. 1971), pp. 3-9.

Gaudy, René. «Cinq Jours à Avignon.» *France Nouvelle*, 24 July 1968, pp. 15-16.

Godard, Colette. «*Alexandra K* d'André Benedetto.» *Le Monde*, 5 Dec. 1975, p. 14.

———. «La Madone de Benedetto.» *Le Monde*, 16 Mar. 1973, p. 16.

———. «Les Régionalismes du Morbihan à Avignon: Géronimo et les Occitans.» *Le Monde*, 27-28 July 1975, p. 15.

Humblot, Catherine. «André Benedetto: Un héros occitan.» *Le Monde*, 1 Dec. 1972, p. 17.

Kourilsky, Françoise. «Avec André Benedetto et les comédiens de la Nouvelle Compagnie d'Avignon.» *Travail Théâtral*, No. 5 (Oct.-Dec. 1971), pp. 10-25.

———. «Avignon 'in' et 'off.'» *Le Nouvel Observateur*, 31 July-6 Aug. 1972, pp. 38-39.

Leonardini, Jean-Pierre. «Catalogue raisonné d'un franc-tireur mordant: André Benedetto.» *A.T.A.C. Informations*, Nov. 1975, pp. 12-17.

———. «Le 23ᵉ Festival d'Avignon; pour quelle destination?» *L'Humanité*, 29 July 1969, p. 7.

Madral, Philippe. «*Zone Rouge, feux interdits* d'André Benedetto.» *L'Humanité*, 30 July 1968, p. 6.

Norès, Dominique. «La S.N.C.F. à dossier ouvert.» *Tribune Socialiste*, 25 July 1969, p. 6.

La Nouvelle Compagnie d'Avignon. «La Dialectique des signes dans notre théâtre.» *Soirées, Revue de la Nouvelle Compagnie d'Avignon*, No. 42 (June-July 1972).

Poirot-Delpech, Bertrand. «Au festival d'Avignon: *Le Petit Train de M. Kamodé*.» *Le Monde*, 2 Aug. 1969, p. 13.

Sandier, Gilles. «Retour aux sources: *Géronimo*.» *La Quinzaine Littéraire*, 1-15 Dec. 1975, p. 28.

Sarrazac, Jean-Pierre. «La Fable et l'aujourd'hui: Notes pour un théâtre épique renouvelé à propos de *Géronimo*.» *Travail Théâtral*, No. 21 (Oct.-Dec. 1975), pp. 48-53.

Saurel, Renée. «Le Double combat d'Alexandra Kollontai.» *Les Temps Modernes*, No. 355 (Jan. 1976), pp. 1373-79.

Sell, Maren and Munster, Arno. «Entretien avec André Benedetto.» *Travail Théâtral*, No. 1 (Oct.-Dec. 1970), pp. 151-53.

Todd, Olivier. «Avignon sur Viet-Nam.» *Le Nouvel Observateur*, 1-7 Feb. 1967, p. 29.

Wahiche, Dominique and Bodin, Pierre. «Un Spectacle, une population.» *Travail Théâtral*, No. 17 (Oct.-Dec. 1974), pp. 113-17.

Théâtre Populaire de Lorraine

«Un Candide exemplaire.» *Journal de Lunéville*, 31 Mar. 1972, p. 3.

Claire, Françoise. «Théâtre, chomage, culture et révolution.» *Tribune Socialiste*, 17 Dec. 1970, p. 18.

Dominique, Laurent. «Compte rendu de *Splendeur et misère de Minette la bonne Lorraine*.» *Le Monde*, 30 June 1969, p. 18.

Ertel, Evelyne. «Essai d'analyse d'un échec: *Noëlle de Joie*.» *Travail Théâtral*, No. 21 (Oct.-Dec. 1975), pp. 86-90.

Godard, Colette. «*Les Immigrés*, par le Théâtre Populaire de Lorraine.» *Le Monde*, 17 June 1972, p. 21.

Kraemer, Jacques. *Les Immigrés*. Paris: P.J. Oswald, 1973.

———. *La Liquidation of M. Joseph K; Jacotte ou Les Plaisirs de la vie quo-*

tidienne. Paris: P.J. Oswald, 1974.

———. *Noëlle de Joie, Les Ciseaux d'Anastasie*. Paris: P.J. Oswald, 1975.

———. «Notre Expérience: Théâtre Populaire de Lorraine.» *Travail Théâtral*, No. 8 (July-Sept. 1972), pp. 57-75.

———. *Parade pour Minette*. n.p. TS., Metz: Le Théâtre Populaire de Lorraine, 1969.

———. *Le Retour de Graully; La Farce du Graully*. Paris: P.J. Oswald, 1973.

———. *Splendeur et misère de Minette la bonne Lorraine*. Paris: Ed. du Seuil, 1970.

Leonardini, Jean-Pierre. «Le Théâtre Populaire de Lorraine devant une promesse de . . . Gascon?» *A.T.A.C. Informations*, June-Aug. 1975, pp. 6-9.

Madral, Philippe. «Pour une nouvelle dramaturgie.» *La Voix de la Moselle*, 11 July 1969, p. 2.

Millon, Martine. «Un Graully qui se mord la queue.» *Travail Théâtral*, No. 17 (Oct.-Dec. 1974), pp. 102-04.

Poirot-Delpech, Bertrand. «Au festival de Nancy.» *Le Monde*, 27 Apr. 1971, p. 26.

Poulet, Jacques. «Compte rendu des *Immigrés*.» *France Nouvelle*, 11 July 1972, pp. 21-22.

«Le Retour du T.P.L.» *Metz, image du mois, magazine de l'agglomération messine*, Jan. 1973, p. 29.

Sandier, Gilles. «Compte rendu de *Splendeur et misère de Minette la bonne Lorraine*.» *La Quinzaine Littéraire*, 16-31 Mar. 1970, p. 28.

Saurel, Renée. «Problèmes du jeune théâtre.» *Les Lettres Françaises*, 23-29 Dec. 1970, p. 22.

———. «Histoire du T.P.L.» n.p. TS., Metz: Théâtre Populaire de Lorraine, 1970.

———. «Programme 1963-1964.» n.p. TS., Metz: Théâtre Populaire de Lorraine, 1963.

Tordjman, Charles. «Le T.P.L. répète *Histoire de l'Oncle Jacob*.» *A.T.A.C. Informations*, May 1976, pp. 34-36.

Zand, Nicole. «Compte rendu de *Splendeur et misère de Minette la bonne Lorraine*.» *Le Monde*, 8-9 Mar. 1970, p. 21.

The Aquarium

Autrusseau, Jacqueline. «De Weitchouang à Vincennes: *Ah Q* de Bernard Chartreux et Jean Jourdheuil par l'Aquarium.» *Travail Théâtral*, No. 22 (Jan.-Mar. 1976), pp. 98-102.

Blanc, Jacques. «*Tu ne voleras point* à la Cartoucherie de Vincennes.» *Libération*, 25 Nov. 1974, pp. 10-11.

Boissieu, Jean. «*Les Evasions de M. Voisin* au festival de Châteauvallon.» *Les Lettres Françaises*, 9-15 Sept. 1970, pp. 17-18.

Chartreux, Bernard and Jourdheuil, Jean. *Ah Q: Ah Kiou, tragédie chinoise d'après Lou Sin*. Paris: Christian Bourgois, 1975.

Cingria, Hélène. «Création collective.» *Le Journal de Genève*, 31 Oct. 1970, p. 11.

Clavet, Jean-Louis. «Le Notaire, sa fiancée, le juge . . . et les journaux.» *Politique Hebdo*, 18 May 1972, p. 7.

Copfermann, Emile. «Les dés pipés.» *Les Lettres Françaises*, 15-21 May 1968, p. 34.

Duguet, Anne-Marie. «Le Théâtre universitaire: son efficacité et son action pratique sur les milieux étudiants.» *Cahiers Théâtre Louvain*, No. 10-11, 1970.

Ertel, Evelyne. «Genèse d'un spectacle: *Gob ou le journal d'un homme normal*, par le Théâtre de l'Aquarium à la Cartoucherie.» *Travail Théâtral*, No. 14 (Jan.-Mar. 1974), pp. 69-75.

Fohr, Anne. «Une Ame de papier, *Gob*, par le Théâtre de l'Aquarium.» *Le Nouvel Observateur*, 24-31 Dec. 1973, p. 9.

Fouche, Christine. «Le Temps du café concert.» *Réforme*, 14 Dec. 1974, p. 31.

Galey, Mathieu. «Compte rendu de *Marchands de Ville*.» *Les Nouvelles Littéraires*, 13-19 Mar. 1972, p. 25.

Gaudy, René. «Théâtre universitaire: Vers la renaissance?» *France Nouvelle*, 24 Jan. 1968, pp. 20-21.

Gautier, Jean-Jacques. «Compte rendu de *Marchands de Ville*.» *Le Figaro*, 26-27 Feb. 1972, p. 28.

Godard, Colette. «Compte rendu des *Evasions de M. Voisin*.» *Le Monde*, 17-18 Jan. 1971, p. 19.

———. «*Gob, ou le journal d'un homme normal*, par l'Aquarium.» *Le Monde*, 6 Dec. 1973, p. 38.

Joliet, Pascal. «Monsieur Gob à la Cartoucherie de Vincennes: les maladies de la presse.» *Libération*, 11 Dec. 1973, p. 10.

Liegeois, Jean-Paul. «Théâtre: *Marchands de Ville* et *40-45*.» *L'Humanité Dimanche*, 15-21 Mar. 1972, p. 21.

Madral, Philippe. «Renaissance du théâtre universitaire: *Les Guerres picrocholines* d'après Rabelais.» *L'Humanité*, 29 Nov. 1967, p. 9.

«*Marchands de Ville*, création du Théâtre de l'Aquarium.» *Bref*, No. 127 (Mar. 1972), pp. 16-19.

Norès, Dominique. «*Ah Q* au T.N.S.» *A.T.A.C. Informations*, Jan. 1976, pp. 15-17.

———. «Le Théâtre de l'Aquarium: Une réflexion sur le rôle du théâtre dans notre société.» *A.T.A.C. Informations*, May 1975, pp. 25-28.

———. «Théâtre universitaire et théâtre politique.» *Tribune Socialiste*, 29 May 1969, pp. 18-19.

Poirot-Delpech, Bertrand. «*Marchands de Ville* par la compagnie de l'Aquarium.» *Le Monde*, 25 Feb. 1972, p. 23.

———. «*La République des honnêtes gens* aux Rencontres du jeune théâtre.» *Le Monde*, 18-19 May 1969, p. 19.

Poulet, Jacques. «Théâtre: Le Caf'Conc de l'Aquarium.» *France Nouvelle*, 30 Dec. 1974, p. 22.

Sandier, Gilles. «Trois Expériences théâtrales: Copi, *La Journée d'une rêveuse*; Arrabal, *Le Cimetière des Voitures*; Rabelais (d'après), *Les Guerres picrocholines*.» *La Quinzaine Littéraire*, 1-15 Feb. 1968, p. 27.

«Théâtre de l'Aquarium.» *Bref*, No. 146 (Feb. 1972), pp. 8-16.

Théâtre de l'Aquarium. *Les Evasions de M. Voisin*. n.p. TS. with technical indications, courtesy of the Aquarium, 1970.

———. *Gob, ou le journal d'un homme normal*, personal tape recording, courtesy of the Aquarium, 1974.

———. *Marchands de Ville*. Paris: Collection du Théâtre National Populaire, 1972.

Yfantis, Anastase. «Le Travail de l'Aquarium dans *Marchands de Ville*.» *Travail Théâtral*, No. 7 (Apr.-June 1972), pp. 149-52.

Zand, Nicole. «Théâtre universitaire: *Les Guerres picrocholines*.» *Le Monde*, 14-15 Jan. 1968, p. 15.

Unpublished Interviews

Robert Abirached	Spring 1974	Summer 1976
André Benedetto	Summer 1975	Summer 1976
Emile Copfermann	Spring 1974	
Anne-Marie Duguet (Aquarium)	Winter 1973	
Jacques Kraemer	Spring 1973	Summer 1975
Jean-Marie Lamblard	Summer 1973	
(Nouvelle Compagnie d'Avignon)		
Sophie Lemasson (Soleil)	Spring 1973	
Philippe Léotard (Soleil)	Spring 1973	
Marcel Maréchal	Winter 1973	
Georges Michel	Spring 1974	
Jacques Nichet (Aquarium)	Fall 1973	Summer 1975
Jean-Claude Penchenat (Soleil)	Summer 1975	